GAME CHANGERS

The Greatest Plays in
OHIO STATE
FOOTBALL HISTORY

David Lee Morgan, Jr.

TRIUMPH
BOOKS

To the most important team in my life, my family.

Triumph Books and colophon are registered trademarks of Random House, Inc.

Library of Congress Cataloging-in-Publication Data

Morgan, David Lee.
  Game changers : the greatest plays in Ohio State football history / David Lee Morgan Jr.
      p. cm.
  ISBN 978-1-60078-266-4
  1. Ohio State University—Football—History. 2. Ohio State Buckeyes (Football team)—History.
I. Title.
  GV958.O35M67 2010
  796.332'630977157—dc22

                                                        2010016571

This book is available in quantity at special discounts for your group or organization. For further information, contact:
  Triumph Books
  542 South Dearborn Street
  Suite 750
  Chicago, Illinois 60605
  (312) 939-3330
  Fax (312) 663-3557
  www.triumphbooks.com

Printed in China
ISBN: 978-1-60078-266-4
Design by Sue Knopf/Patricia Frey
Page production by Patricia Frey
Photos courtesy of Getty Images unless otherwise noted

Contents

Foreword

To say that Ohio State Football is a big thing in the lives of Buckeyes fans is maybe the biggest understatement you might ever come across. Those who follow the Scarlet and Gray plan their social calendars around the football schedule. You should hear the grief that couples who plan weddings during Football Saturdays get. When a spring game, a glorified practice, draws more than 90,000 people to pack Ohio Stadium—well, that should tell you enough!

From football seasons that predate most of us, there are the special players who have made Ohio State Football what it is. A young man from Columbus East High School by the name of Chic Harley starred for Ohio State when the Buckeyes played at old Ohio Field. It was Harley's exploits that prompted the need for the gigantic structure that now sits along the Olentangy River, a football shrine affectionately called "the Horseshoe." There is a reverence that accompanies the mentions of Heisman Trophy–winning names such as Les Horvath, Vic Janowicz, Hopalong Cassady, Eddie George, and Troy Smith. There is a pride displayed by Buckeyes fans that Ohio State lays claim to the only two-time Heisman winner, Archie Griffin, a man whose humility and dedication to his university match his exploits on the field.

Then when the name "Woody" is mentioned, it takes the romance of this sport in this Midwest state to an even higher level. The success of Woody Hayes' teams at Ohio State, his potential for monumental outbursts, and his legacy of teaching the all-around importance of "paying forward," has earned him a special place in the hearts and minds of Buckeyes fans—past, present, and future.

That's not to mention the special plays, or seasons. Folks still wax nostalgic about the 1950 "Snow Bowl" game with Michigan. They gnash their teeth over the decision by Ohio State's Faculty Council in 1961 to veto a Rose Bowl berth. Bring up the magical 1968 season, when the Buckeyes' "Super Sophomores" shocked college football by running the table and defeating USC for the national title, to the delight of many. Listen to folks tell you about the game-winning TD pass from Joe Germaine to David Boston to beat Arizona State in the 1997 Rose Bowl. There are the many stories about the 2002 campaign; people fondly recalling cliff-hangers against Cincinnati, Wisconsin, Purdue, Illinois, and Michigan. There's not a Buckeye fan around who can't tell you where they were when Miami's fourth-down pass attempt fell incomplete in the game's second overtime, as Ohio State dethroned the Hurricanes to win their most recent national title.

Ohio State Football is truly a religion, and Saturdays are the holy days of obligation for those who don scarlet and gray paraphernalia, paint their faces, and spend months planning their tailgate parties. While many Ohio State players, coaches, plays, and seasons can be looked at as game changers, to say they've been life changers to Buckeyes fans isn't too far off the mark.

—Paul Keels

Ohio State broadcaster
Paul Keels. *Photo courtesy
of Chance Brockway*

Spectacular Catches

January 1, 2010

California Dreamin'

Buckeyes Bust the Ducks to Win First Rose Bowl Since 1997

The 2010 Rose Bowl was a must-win for the Buckeyes. There was no doubt about it: Ohio State *had* to beat Oregon.

In 2009 Ohio State went into the Tostitos Fiesta Bowl against favored Texas and lost 24–21 on a Longhorns' 26-yard touchdown pass from quarterback Colt McCoy to Quan Cosby with 16 seconds left. It was a heartbreaking defeat for Ohio State. Most felt that the Buckeyes outplayed Texas until those last 16 seconds.

Sure, critics continued to fuel the "Ohio State-can't-win-the-big-one" flame after the loss, but supporters were happy with the moral victory and the fact that the Buckeyes held their own against the McCoy-led Longhorns.

The reality in 2010, however, was that Coach Jim Tressel and the Buckeyes couldn't settle for a moral victory. In the Rose Bowl, a loss, even against the high-powered PAC-10 Champs Oregon, led by quarterback Jeremiah Masoli, would have been devastating to Tressel and the program.

Fortunately, Ohio State never left any doubt in a 26–17 win over the No. 7–ranked Ducks in front of 93,963 fans. The Buckeyes were ranked eighth.

Tight end Jake Ballard makes an incredible leaping catch on third down in the fourth quarter of the 2010 Rose Bowl.

"We needed it, just for the Big Ten as a whole," said Ohio State sophomore quarterback Terrelle Pryor, who was magnificent in leading Ohio State's offense. He threw 23-of-37 for a career-high 266 yards and two touchdowns. "I know we battled [Big Ten teams] all year long, but we're also playing for each other because it's a rep. We're playing for each other, and when schools like Penn State are playing in other bowls, it's a reputation for us. It was huge for us to get over that hump and win this game, and we've just got to keep on winning."

Ohio State linebacker Kurt Coleman, who was one of the leaders on the Buckeyes' defense all season long, said it was a crucial victory as well.

"These four years have been great, and I think after every loss that we've had at the end of every bowl has been a learning experience and last year we were so close to winning, and I think that was one of our biggest motivation factors going into the off-season," Coleman said.

The Buckeyes dominated the game on both sides of the ball and completely shut down Masoli and the Ducks. Oregon entered the game averaging 424.67 yards in total offense but were held to just 260 total yards and 12 first downs.

Game Details

Ohio State 26, Oregon 17

Ohio State	10	6	3	7	**26**
Oregon	0	10	7	0	**17**

Date: January 1, 2010

Team Records: Ohio State 11–2, Oregon 10–3

Scoring Plays:

OSU—Saine 13-yard pass from Pryor (Pettrey PAT)

OSU—Barclay 19-yard FG

UO—Flint 24-yard FG

UO—Blount 3-yard run (Flint PAT)

OSU—Barclay 30-yard FG

OSU—Pettrey 45-yard FG

UO—Masoli 1-yard run (Flint PAT)

OSU—Barclay 38-yard FG

OSU—Posey 17-yard pass from Pryor (Pettrey PAT)

"Well, I thought our guys prepared extremely well, and we were going to make sure that he wasn't running scot-free," Tressel said about the defensive scheme against Masoli. "He did get in the end zone, and he did break a couple in there. I thought he made a couple nice throws."

Quarterback Terrelle Pryor was a crucial force in the Buckeyes' Rose Bowl win over the Oregon Ducks.

"Pryor" Injury Doesn't Hinder QB

You saw it in the opening drive of the 2010 Rose Bowl. Ohio State quarterback Terrelle Pryor eluded several Oregon would-be tacklers, scrambled to the outside, and scampered for a big gain before running out of bounds.

During that run, Pryor had a noticeable limp. It had been a concern leading up to the game: he was bothered by a slight tear in the posterior cruciate ligament (PCL) in his left knee. Yet he never let the injury take away from his performance.

"It was bothering me," Pryor said. "I had a little PCL injury and I was just trying to hide it a little bit and trying to ignore it. That didn't matter. For these seniors...we just wanted to send the seniors out with a win."

Pryor was sensational in the win and had his best performance of his collegiate career.

"Don't get me wrong, as a quarterback you don't like running the ball," he said. "It's kind of like being selfish, but you know, that's not what we need. This is a big-time organization, Ohio State, and if you have to run the ball to win the game, that's what you do."

Oregon coach Chip Kelly was asked if he was surprised that the normally conservative Tressel opened up things offensively, right from the start.

"It was surprising to us," Kelly said. "We felt watching their last couple of games where they didn't throw it very much and were rather conservative, they came in and opened it up, and obviously Terrelle beat us."

We needed it, just for the Big Ten as a whole.

—TERRELLE PRYOR

But you know, we played our defense. Our kids prepared extremely hard on defense. We've been saying that all year long. They really put the time in and the effort in. They play together, and they're a tight bunch. They can put pressure on you, and if you can put pressure on the quarterback, especially in Oregon's system, as good as Masoli is, if you can keep a little heat on him, it's going to give you a lot better chances."

Coleman said the win proved that Ohio State could still compete with anyone in the nation—and win, despite the previous bowl woes.

"There are some games that we just didn't execute, and I think you go back to national championship games [in 2006 and 2007] and we just didn't execute well enough," Coleman said. "[Against Oregon,] we played our best ball, I think, throughout the whole year. That's what you have to do. We came to show up in this game, and we have the talent to run with anybody, but [today] we showed up and we played our brand of ball."

Taking a page from Tressel's philosophy, Pryor said he felt blessed and grateful for the opportunity to be put in such a rewarding situation.

"I'm just so glad to be a part of this team, how hard we work, and where we want to be. And these seniors, we needed to come out and win for these seniors," Pryor said. "The offense did a great job to help out the defense, because our defense, they've been carrying a lot this year sometimes, and we're just glad we got out there and tried to help them out as much as we could, and we did, pretty good…I just thank God I have the teammates like Kurt and the seniors, and I wish them all well."

You won't find many people in this locker room that are surprised he played like that.
—WIDE RECEIVER DANE SANZENBACHER

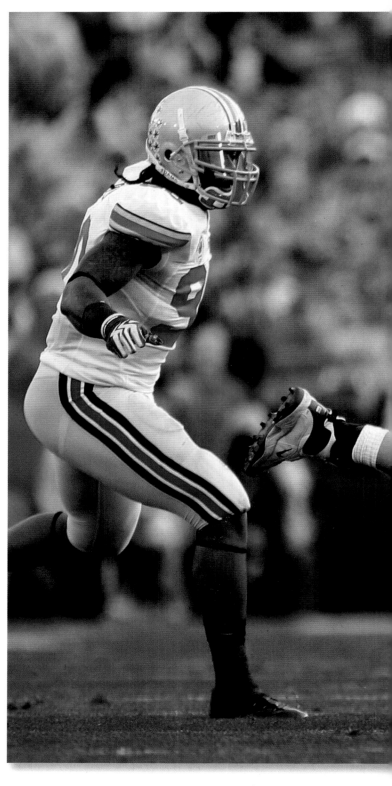

Linebacker Russ Homan (51) came up with a clutch interception in the game.

September 9, 2006

Burnt Like Texas Toast

After Losing to the Longhorns in 2005 in Columbus, the Buckeyes Serve It Up in Texas in 2006

There were so many words to describe Ohio State's 24–7 win at Texas. But there's one word that expresses it best: *dominating*. And it *was* a dominating performance by Ohio State at Royal-Texas Memorial Stadium. The Longhorns entered the game ranked No. 2 in the country; Ohio State was ranked No. 1.

In a defensive struggle through the first quarter, Ohio State drew first blood on a 14-yard touchdown reception from quarterback Troy Smith to wide receiver Anthony Gonzalez for a 7–0 lead. Texas tied the score 7–7 on a two-yard touchdown pass from Colt McCoy to Billy Pittman with 1:55 left before halftime.

The way both defenses played for most of the first half, most of the 89,422 fans probably thought that would be the halftime score. But the Buckeyes, led offensively by Smith, came alive in the final minute of the first half. Smith hit Ted Ginn Jr. on a 29-yard touchdown pass with just 16 seconds left before halftime, giving Ohio State a 7-point lead. Ginn Jr. used his exceptional speed to get behind Texas defensive back Aaron Ross and never broke stride as he hauled in Smith's pass and crossed the goal line for a monumental score.

It seemed that Ginn Jr.'s touchdown completely knocked the life out of the Longhorns. They never recovered. In fact, after Pittman's touchdown for Texas late in the second quarter, the Longhorns were held scoreless the rest of the game.

"Anytime you hold a team like Texas to seven points in their own stadium is incredible," Tressel said.

Smith finished with 269 passing yards and two touchdowns. Gonzalez, meanwhile, had caught eight passes for 142 yards, both

Ted Ginn Jr.'s second-quarter touchdown reception was the turning point in the Buckeyes' victory over the Texas Longhorns.

career highs, against a defense concentrating on Ginn, who finished with five catches for 97 yards.

"It's a sign of how Troy has matured," Gonzalez said about Smith's poise in the win. "It's what we've come to expect of him and what he's come to expect of himself."

Meanwhile, Ohio State's defense, led by defensive end Vernon Gholston and an up-and-coming linebacker

We came in here and beat the No. 2 team in the country and the defending national champion in front of their home crowd.

—VERNON GHOLSTON

Wide receiver Anthony Gonzalez also got in on the action, scoring a first-quarter touchdown and finishing the day with a career-high 142 receiving yards.

Hooking the 'Horns

Before you can understand the magnitude of Ohio State's 24–7 win at Texas in 2006, you have to go back and examine the gut-wrenching loss to Texas at the "Shoe" in the previous season.

In 2005 the Longhorns, led by Heisman Trophy runner-up Vince Young, defeated Ohio State 25–22. Texas went on to win the national championship and the Buckeyes ended the season 10–2, including an impressive 34–20 win against Notre Dame in the Fiesta Bowl.

The Buckeyes struggled with a quarterback controversy at the start of the 2005 season. Troy Smith sat out the season opener serving an NCAA suspension. Justin Zwick got the start and looked solid in a 34–14 win against Miami University. Smith's suspension served, Tressel used both quarterbacks the following week against Texas in Columbus.

"I remember going into the Texas game in 2005 with a lot of uncertainty," Zwick said. "I didn't know how the rotation was going to be, and neither did Troy."

Heading into the 2006 season, Ohio State's defense, which had to replace nine starters, looked like a veteran team in Texas. The Buckeyes held the Longhorns to just seven points and Texas entered the game having scored at least 40 points in 12 consecutive games.

"We've been winning so much, I forgot how it feels to lose," Texas wide receiver Limas Sweed said about the 24–7 loss to Ohio State.

And by the way Ohio State played, it looked like the Buckeyes never forgot about that loss to Texas in Columbus the year before.

named James Laurinaitis, never let McCoy and the Longhorns establish any substantial drive. McCoy threw for 154 yards, a touchdown, and an interception.

"We came in here and beat the No. 2 team in the country and the defending national champion in front of their home crowd," Gholston said. "We showed everybody what we can do."

But very quickly, Tressel, in typical Tressel fashion, made sure his players didn't get too excited about the win, because there were still 10 games remaining in the regular season.

"We haven't claimed anything yet," Tressel said. "We still have to go back to the Horseshoe and keep winning games."

Well, after the Texas win, the Buckeyes reeled off 10 consecutive wins en route to Tressel's second BCS national championship appearance since 2001.

Game Details

Ohio State 24 • Texas 7

Ohio State	7	7	3	7	**24**
Texas	0	7	0	0	**7**

Date: September 9, 2006

Team Records: Ohio State 2–0, Texas 1–1

Scoring Plays:

OSU—Gonzalez 14-yard pass from Smith (Pettrey PAT)

UT—B. Pittman 2-yard pass from McCoy (Johnson PAT)

OSU—Ginn Jr. 29-yard pass from Smith (Pettrey PAT)

OSU—Pettrey 31-yard FG

OSU—A. Pittman 2-yard run (Pettrey PAT)

September 30, 1995

Regis Philbin Speechless? No Way!

Buckeyes Silence Famous Notre Dame Alum with Big Play

The final score was 45–26, Ohio State over Notre Dame. It was a victory delivered in convincing fashion. Running back Eddie George had an impressive game, rushing 32 times for 207 yards and two touchdowns.

Buckeyes quarterback Bobby Hoying had a productive night as well, completing 14-of-22 passes for 272 yards and four touchdowns.

"The whole community got involved with this game so much," said Ohio State quarterback Bobby Hoying. "We're so happy to win it for us and the community, the city of Columbus, and the Ohio State fans. It's something we can look back on and say, 'We beat Notre Dame.'"

The No. 6-ranked Buckeyes faced the No. 15 Irish in the comfy confines of the Horseshoe in Columbus, but in the first half, things weren't going the Buckeyes' way at all. Notre Dame quarterback Ron Powlus and running back Randy Kinder helped the Irish jump out to an early 10–0 lead in the second quarter, then Notre Dame led 17–7 with 4:31 left before halftime.

Ohio State cut the lead to three with 44 seconds left in the second quarter on a 17-yard touchdown pass from Bobby Hoying to Dimitrious Stanley. That touchdown proved to be a momentum changer.

"The touchdown just before the half was big for them, I'm sure," Notre Dame coach Lou Holtz said after the game.

Yet, midway through the third quarter, Notre Dame extended their lead to 20–14, with a 22-yard field goal by Kevin Kopka. The Buckeyes answered back with a 15-yard touchdown pass from Hoying to Rickey Dudley. It was Ohio State's first lead of the game, one they would never relinquish.

A few minutes later, Ohio State was deep in their own own territory, at a pivotal point in the game and facing a third-and-3 situation. ABC went to sideline reporter Lynn Swann for a quick interview. He was standing with famed Notre Dame alumni and television personality Regis Philbin. "This man has to be the biggest Notre Dame fan in all the country," Swann said, turning to Philbin. "I know you're a little disappointed right now."

Ohio State's Terry Glenn streaks past Irish defender Allen Rossum. The reception was good for 82 yards and six points. *Photo courtesy of AP Images*

Philbin, who was still energetic, said, "You know, ever since you guys called me down here [to the sideline], we've taken a turn for the worse. I'm really aggravated, Lynn. I'm sitting up there and we're winning. I come down here, we're losing."

"Why do you think that is, Regis?" Swann asked.

"Breaks, big breaks," Philbin said. "You gotta admit that."

Philbin was right about that. Two fumbles and an interception by Notre Dame led to 21 Ohio State points in the second half.

Swann continued talking with Philbin as the camera went back to the action on the field. Hoying went under center as viewers listened to Philbin continue his sideline interview with Swann. "But you watch. We're coming back. We're going to bottle them up now. We got a lock on it. We're going to win."

Just as Philbin finished his sentence, Hoying took the snap, dropped back, and hit wide receiver Terry Glenn with a perfect pass between two defenders at Ohio State's 29. From there, Glenn turned on his world-class speed and outran three of Notre Dame's defensive backs, including

The final score at Ohio Stadium. *Photo courtesy of Ohio State University Photo Archives*

Allen Rossum, a nationally ranked NCAA sprinter, and raced 82 yards for a touchdown, giving Ohio State a 28–20 lead. Glenn's touchdown proved to be the game winner.

After that score, Philbin, still on the sideline with Swann but now back on camera said, "We're still coming back…We're going to win."

But on the television screen, all you saw was Hoying running down the field raising his hands in the air. And all you heard was the booming, driving, rhythmic, and mesmerizing sound of *The Buckeye Battle Cry* being played by "The Best Damn Band in the Land."

With that Glenn touchdown, Ohio State took control, outscoring Notre Dame 17–6 the rest of the way, and the Buckeyes never looked back.

Game Details

Ohio State 45 • Notre Dame 26

Notre Dame	0	17	3	6	**26**
Ohio State	0	14	14	17	**45**

Date: September 30, 1995

Team Records: Ohio State 4–0, Notre Dame 3–2

Scoring Plays:

ND—Kopka 20-yard FG

ND—Kinder 3-yard run (Kopka PAT)

OSU—Glenn 10-yard pass from Hoying (Jo. Jackson PAT)

ND—Kinder 7-yard run (Kopka PAT)

OSU—Stanley 17-yard pass from Hoying (Jo. Jackson PAT)

ND—Kopka 22-yard field goal

OSU—Dudley 15-yard pass from Hoying (Jo. Jackson kick)

OSU—Glenn 82-yard pass from Hoying (Jackson PAT)

OSU—George 5-yard run (Jackson PAT)

ND—Kinder 13-yard run (run failed)

OSU—George 3-yard run (Jackson PAT)

OSU—Jackson 35-yard FG

> **W**e got a lock on it. We're going to win.
> —REGIS PHILBIN

A Tale of Turnovers

As demoralizing as Terry Glenn's 82-yard touchdown catch-and-run was to Notre Dame, it was an earlier touchdown catch by tight end Rickey Dudley that helped give the Buckeyes the lead for good. Quarterback Bobby Hoying found Dudley in the middle of the field and Dudley fought off several Irish defenders on his way into the end zone.

That touchdown was the result of one of many Notre Dame turnovers committed on the day. Irish punt returner Emmett Mosley misjudged a kick with Notre Dame leading 20–14 and the ball was recovered by Ohio State deep in Irish territory.

"When I went to catch it, I felt my man right there, and I figured it would hit him if I didn't catch it," Mosley told a reporter from the student newspaper, the *Observer*. "But it turned out it was one of their men right near me."

It didn't take the Buckeyes long to capitalize on Notre Dame's turnover. The Buckeyes scored three plays later on Dudley's touchdown catch.

Dudley only caught two passes for 35 yards that afternoon, but that 15-yard touchdown reception was crucial. It gave Ohio State a 21–20 lead, a lead they never relinquished. Glenn caught four passes for 128 yards.

Meanwhile, Notre Dame big-play wide receiver Derrick Mayes put up numbers. He caught five passes for 125 yards. But he wasn't able to get into the end zone. Irish running back Randy Kinder and kicker Kevin Kopka combined for all of Notre Dame's scoring. Kinder scored on three rushing touchdowns and Kopka kicked two field goals and converted on two extra points.

Anthony Gonzalez proves
why he is uncatchable.

November 19, 2005

"The Catch"

Clutch Reception By Anthony Gonzalez Secures OSU
Upset of Michigan at the Big House

Most Ohio State fans simply call it "the Catch." Wide
receiver Anthony Gonzalez' acrobatic 26-yard reception
against Michigan at the "Big House" was pure clutch play. It
helped set up Antonio Pittman's game-winning three-yard
touchdown run with just 24 seconds left, in a 25–21 win.

Gonzalez called his catch and the game-winning drive orchestrated
by quarterback Troy Smith something else. "Quiet confidence...that's a
term I would use," Gonzalez told the *Mansfield Journal*. "It was a relaxed,
'hey, we're about to win a football game' [mood]."

Ohio State, ranked No. 9 at the time, trailed 17th-ranked Michigan
21–12 with 7:49 left to play after a 19-yard Garrett Rivas field goal. But
the Buckeyes didn't buckle. They wasted no time cutting into the lead.
Smith marched the offense down the field and threw a 26-yard touchdown pass to Santonio Holmes to cut Michigan's lead to two with 6:40 still
left on the clock. Ohio State's defense came up with a stop on Michigan's
next possession, and instead of trying a tough field goal into the wind, the
Wolverines punted. The Buckeyes took possession at their own 12 with
4:18 remaining.

Several minutes later, Smith and Gonzalez got together for one of the
most memorable plays in Buckeyes history. Ohio State had the ball first-
and-10 at Michigan's 31 with 47 seconds remaining. Smith took the snap

from the shotgun formation and Gonzalez was lined up by himself on the right.

Smith felt pressure, so he started to take a few steps toward the line of scrimmage to avoid the rush from the outside. At that moment, Michigan inside linebacker David Harris slid off his block and surged up the middle. Harris had a clear path to Smith. Harris dove at Smith's ankles but Smith danced out of Harris' grasp, dropped back, and rolled to his right. As he rolled, he threw off-balance and across his body. It was a pass that cornerback Grant Mason, who was running with Gonzalez, didn't see coming.

"Guys came off the edge, and I was just trying to stay alive," Smith told the Associated Press. "I saw [Gonzalez] pop open down the sideline, and I just tried to get him the ball as fast as I could."

Game Details

Ohio State 25 • Michigan 21

Ohio State	6	6	0	13	**25**
Michigan	0	7	11	3	**21**

Date: November 19, 2005

Team Records: Ohio State 9–2, Michigan 7–4

Scoring Plays:

OSU—Smith 4-yard run (kick failed)

OSU—Huston 47-yard field goal

UM—Avant 2-yard pass from Henne (Rivas PAT)

OSU—Huston 25-yard FG

UM—Rivas 27-yard FG

UM—Grady 2-yard run (Henne run)

UM—Rivas 19-yard FG

OSU—Holmes 26-yard pass from Smith (Huston PAT)

OSU—Pittman 3-yard run (pass failed)

Gonzo

One of the things that made Ohio State special during the 2005 season was that a handful of key skill players came from the same area. Anthony Gonzalez, Troy Smith, and Ted Ginn Jr. all came from Cleveland.

So when Gonzalez caught the 26-yard pass from Smith to help set up the game-winning touchdown against Michigan in Ann Arbor, one of the first players downfield to greet Gonzalez was Ginn Jr. The two players were friendly rivals in Cleveland. Gonzalez went to Division I perennial power St. Ignatius High School and Ginn Jr. played for his father, Ted Ginn Sr., at Glenville High, a perennial powerhouse public school. Smith also attended Glenville and was Ginn Jr.'s teammate and close friend.

Gonzalez and Ginn Jr., were also friendly rivals on the track, two of the fastest sprinters in the state in their senior years.

Gonzalez won a football state championship his junior year at Ignatius and was named Co-Defensive Player of the Year while at Ignatius. He caught 71 passes for 1,873 yards and 21 touchdowns during his tenure there. He was also a four-year letterman in track and a state finalist as a junior and senior.

At Ohio State, Gonzalez caught 87 passes for 1,286 yards (14.8 yards per catch average) and 13 touchdowns.

Gonzalez's brother Joe was a safety for Indiana in the early 2000s. Their father, Eduardo, played football at Michigan. Gonzalez was the 32nd overall pick in the 2007 NFL Draft, selected by the Indianapolis Colts.

The pass was high and Gonzalez made a leaping grab just before Mason turned around to look for the ball. The play was incredible; it showed outstanding concentration and athletic ability from Smith and Gonzalez.

"A lot of youngsters watching this game will be in their yards on Thanksgiving weekend making the same moves [Smith] made and getting open in the pile of leaves [like Gonzalez]," Tressel said after the game. "That's the fun of college football at this time of year."

Michigan defensive tackle Pat Massey said, "Troy is probably the best we've seen. Troy was a difference maker out there."

Smith was 27-of-37 for 300 yards, one touchdown, and did not throw an interception.

"I just think we wanted it more than those guys," Holmes said after the game. "I give all the style points to Gonzo for that catch. The way he went up for that ball, I commend him for what he did."

The loss put Michigan coach Lloyd Carr's record at 1–4 against Tressel.

"There is nothing that can make you feel better after losing this game," a dejected Carr said afterward.

Antonio Pittman scores the game-winning touchdown in Ohio State's 25–21 win over the Wolverines in Ann Arbor.

December 28, 1985

Hands Like Glue

Cris Carter's One-Handed Catch Still Amazes Teammates

Ohio State defeated Brigham Young University 10–7 in the 1985 Citrus Bowl. The game was a defensive battle. In fact, the lone touchdown for the Buckeyes in the victory was Larry Kolic's 14-yard interception return early in the third quarter.

Ohio State quarterback Jim Karsatos probably thought he had seen it all during his years as the starting quarterback at Ohio State. And then he saw what he later described as the greatest catch he'd ever seen.

It came as Karsatos was trying to make nothing out of nothing. He was being pressured hard by BYU's defense. When nothing is there, quarterbacks are coached to throw the ball out of bounds instead of trying to force a pass that could wind up a mistake. Seeing nothing develop, Karsatos threw what he thought was a pass that would sail out of bounds.

But Cris Carter had a different idea. When a ball is thrown in his direction, he's going to try to catch the ball, no matter what. And that's what Carter did with Karsatos' apparent "throwaway."

In the book *Buckeye Madness: The Glorious, Tumultuous, Behind-the-Scenes Story of Ohio State Football* by Joe Menzer, Karsatos recounted the play:

Cris Carter's circus catch kept the drive alive and helped the Buckeyes edge BYU.

I was getting chased by Jason Buck, who was way faster than I was. I was getting near the sideline and I thought, *Let's not take a sack here. Let's just throw the ball away.* I saw Cris kind of tiptoeing the sidelines and I thought, *I'll just throw this over his head and we won't get intentional grounding and we can come back for the next play.*

So I wind it up and let it go high and outside, and Jason kind of rolled me out of bounds. When I finally saw it on film, [Cris] was tiptoeing on the sidelines and he jumped up and caught the ball left-handed by the point of the football, at least a yard out of bounds. Then he somehow levitated back in bounds to get both of his feet in bounds. I swear to this day that he actually levitated to get back in bounds. When I saw it on film, it just blew me away.

Running back John Wooldridge saw if from a different perspective. He had the bulk of the carries in that game since Keith Byars was out with a foot injury and Vince Workman had been benched by coach Earle Bruce for his issues with holding onto the ball.

Game Details

Ohio State 10 • Brigham Young 7

Brigham Young	0	7	0	0	**7**
Ohio State	0	3	7	0	**10**

Date: December 28, 1985

Team Records: Brigham Young 11–3, Ohio State 9–3

Scoring Plays:

OSU—Spangler 47-yard FG

BYU—Miles 38-yard pass from Bosco (Webster PAT)

OSU—Kolic 14-yard interception (Spangler PAT)

Wooldridge was pass-protecting as Carter ran his route and Karsatos dropped back, so Wooldridge was able to see the play develop. "I knew the defense was closing in on [Jim]," Wooldridge said. "He stepped back, and after seeing film, I saw that he was just trying to wing it out of bounds."

With Carter almost glued to the white stripe of the sideline, he leaned his entire body out of bounds, while keeping his feet in bounds. "Cris had hands like baseball gloves," Wooldridge said. "He stretched that arm out with one hand, and it was funny because there were people on the sideline who were actually ready to catch the ball thinking it was going out of bounds. But the ball hit Cris in the hand and it stuck like glue."

The circus catch kept the drive alive.

"I think we were able to get a field goal on that drive, so that was a very important play," Wooldridge said. "I remember I got stopped on fourth and goal at the 1, and BYU's defense really smacked me in the mouth. So plays like Cris' catch and Kolic's big interception return really gave us the margin of victory that we needed."

> **W**hen I saw it on film it just blew me away.
>
> **—JIM KARSATOS**

Everybody Loves Cris

If you were an Ohio State football fan during the Woody Hayes era, you knew his famous philosophy was "three yards and a cloud of dust." That changed just a bit when head coach Earl Bruce, a Hayes protégé, recruited a young man from Middletown, Ohio. That young man was Cris Carter. He was an outstanding two-sport athlete who starred in basketball and football. As the story goes, the reason Carter accepted the scholarship offer from Coach Bruce was because his mother was a huge Buckeyes fan.

Carter initially planned to pursue both basketball and football in Columbus, but after making an immediate impact his freshman year he decided to concentrate on football. Carter had a breakout season in his sophomore year, and during his junior year he was one of the best receivers in the Big Ten.

He lost his senior year of eligibility after the discovery that he had secretly signed a contract with notorious sports agent Norby Walters. He entered the 1987 NFL supplemental draft and was selected by the Philadelphia Eagles. After playing three years, he was a surprise release during the 1990 preseason. Carter later admitted that Eagles coach Buddy Ryan released him because of alcohol and drug abuse, but Carter credited Ryan with helping him turn his life around. Carter went on to play 13 more years in the NFL, with the Minnesota Vikings and the Miami Dolphins, before retiring in 2002.

After a successful career at Ohio State, Cris Carter went on to be a top receiver in the NFL. *Photo courtesy of AP Images*

September 23, 2006

Patience Is a Virtue

Quarterback Troy Smith's Pass to Brian Robiskie Is a Backbreaker for the Nittany Lions

It was yet another one of the many incredible plays that Ohio State quarterback Troy Smith came up with in his amazing career with the Buckeyes. But this particular play, a 37-yard touchdown pass to wide receiver Brian Robiskie in a 28–6 win against Penn State at Ohio Stadium, was precious—no, priceless—because it illustrated the pure athleticism that Smith possessed and exemplified his ability to produce big plays in big games. It was a Heisman Trophy highlight for the Cleveland native.

With the top-ranked Buckeyes battling No. 24 Penn State and leading 7–3 in the early minutes of the fourth quarter, Smith knew he needed to spark his team. The Nittany Lions were hanging around much too long. And all it would have taken was a big play on Penn State's part to change the momentum of the game.

Instead, it was Smith who delivered that big play, one of the most spectacular ever by an Ohio State quarterback. The Buckeyes had the ball at Penn State's 37 on second-and-9. Smith, in shotgun formation, took the snap and started to roll to his right. He was pressured as he rolled

near the sideline, but instead of throwing the ball away and facing third down, he decided to reverse field and scramble to his left to look for an open receiver.

It wasn't a decision Tressel, a former high school and college quarterback himself, wanted to see one of his quarterbacks make, but then this was Troy Smith. The potential for something positive happening in such an improvisational situation was always a possibility.

Still, while scrambling, Smith had run back into Ohio State territory, almost to the Buckeyes' 45. Then Smith saw what he was looking for: Robiskie downfield, *way* downfield. Robiskie never gave up on his quarterback, just as Smith never gave up on his receivers.

"I just wanted to work to get open, because I know he can always make a play," Robiskie said about Smith.

Smith unleashed a rocket that seemed to take an eternity to get down the field but it landed right in the arms of Robiskie, who got behind Penn State defenders Tony Davis and Anthony Scirrotto, and caught the ball in the end zone for the score.

"The first read wasn't there," Smith said after the game to the Associated Press. "I tried to come back and look to the other side of the field, but it was kind of clogged and

One on one, wide receiver Brian Robiskie was unbeatable. *Photo courtesy of AP Images*

Brian Robiskie

Brian Robiskie, the son of NFL assistant coach Terry Robiskie, became known for making clutch catches during his career at Ohio State. He saw little time at wide receiver as a freshman, but coach Jim Tressel liked Robiskie's speed and abilities, so Robiskie played in all 12 games that season as a special teams player. During his sophomore year, Robiskie played in all 13 games and started five. One of those notable games came against Penn State. He also caught the game-wining pass, a 13-yard reception with 5:39 left in the game against Michigan that season in a 42–39 victory.

In his junior year, Robiskie led the Buckeyes with 55 catches for 935 yards and 11 touchdowns and won the Paul Warfield Award, which is handed out to the team's Most Outstanding Receiver.

During Robiskie's senior season, with highly touted freshman quarterback Terrelle Pryor at the helm, Robiskie's numbers decreased slightly, but he was still selected as the 36th overall pick in the 2008 NFL draft by the Cleveland Browns.

"We think he's ready to play right away," Browns general manager George Kokinis said about his selection of Robiskie. "Receiver is tough position to come into in the NFL. It's a lot to learn. It's reading on the fly, it's running routes, it's knowing how to position your body. He went to a big-time university and he was well coached there. He understands it. He's grown up with it. That's important as you're making the transition at that spot."

> You can't give up big plays in a game like this.
>
> —JOE PATERNO

crowded, and I just tried to improvise and keep things going. The Penn State defender was making ground on me."

Talking about Robiskie's route adjustment and catch, Smith said, "He stayed with me and went up and made a great catch." Smith was quick to give credit to the rest of his guys, as well. "The mark of a championship-caliber team is to keep plugging away, keep going, keep going, keep going, and we did a great job up front. And the defense, what can you say?"

Penn State coach Joe Paterno was sick with the stomach flu and, no doubt, Smith's play didn't help his condition. But the always-classy Paterno gave Smith his due.

"Smith made a super play," Paterno acknowledged. "You can't give up big plays in a game like this."

Smith's pass to Robiskie was a backbreaker for the Nittany Lions, who never recovered. The touchdown helped the Buckeyes outscore Penn State 21–3 in the fourth quarter. Two of Ohio State's scores came courtesy of the defense, both huge interception returns for touchdowns (a 61-yard return by Malcolm Jenkins and a 55-yard return by Antonio Smith).

"Whenever your defense holds people to six points, you ought to have a chance," Tressel said. "When your defense scores two touchdowns, it's pretty darn good."

Robiskie shows his pure athleticism in a game against Troy.

Game Details

Ohio State 28 • Penn State 6

Penn State	0	3	0	3	**6**
Ohio State	0	0	7	21	**28**

Date: September 23, 2006

Team Records: Ohio State 4–0, Penn State 2–2

Scoring Plays:

PSU—Kelly 21-yard FG

OSU—Pittman 12-yard run (Pettrey PAT)

OSU—Robiskie 37-yard pass from Smith (Pettrey PAT)

PSU—Kelly 23-yard FG

OSU—Jenkins 61-yard interception return (Pettrey PAT)

OSU—Smith 55-yard interception return (Pretorius PAT)

September 29, 1979

An "Artful" Display

Ohio State Quarterback Art Schlichter Leads Buckeyes
on Impressive Game-Winning Drive

A sophomore quarterback from the Midwest wasn't supposed to do this. He wasn't supposed to go into Los Angeles Memorial Coliseum against the UCLA Bruins and orchestrate a game-winning drive to near perfection, but that's just what he did.

And that "he" was Buckeyes quarterback Art Schlichter, who, with his poised and steady play, helped Ohio State to a 17–13 win over the Bruins. Schlichter hit tight end Paul Campbell with a perfect two-yard touchdown pass with just 46 seconds left, stunning and silencing the crowd of 47,228 fans at the Coliseum.

The Buckeyes had not held the lead in the entire game until that point. They fell behind 10–0 late in the first quarter, but cut UCLA's lead to 10–7 on a 34-yard touchdown run by Calvin Murray midway through the second quarter and that was the score at halftime.

Midway through the third quarter, Ohio State tied the score at 10–10 on a 24-yard field goal by Vlade Janakievski. But UCLA took a 13–10 lead late in the game on a 39-yard field goal by Peter Boermeester.

As for Schlichter's touchdown pass to Campbell, Coach Earle Bruce made the call from the sideline: it was going to be "Pass Play 21." The play was set up perfectly. Schlichter's job was to fake a handoff to Murray, then roll out to the right and either run the ball in the end zone or look to throw the ball. The play developed just as Bruce had planned. At the snap, it looked as though Murray was going to take the handoff and try to plow his way into the end zone. Instead, Schlichter let the defense pursue him long enough for Campbell to get alone in the end zone. Then Schlichter tossed a perfect strike for the game-winning touchdown. The Ohio State offensive unit went 80 yards in eight plays, with Schlichter going 6-for-6 on that drive.

Quarterback Art Schlichter is carried away by the victory parade. *Photo courtesy of AP Images*

The Highs and Lows of Art Schlichter

The career of Ohio State quarterback Art Schlichter on the field was just as chronicled as his much-talked-about career off the field. A star athlete at Miami Trace High School in Bloomingburg, Ohio, Schlichter was a four-year starter at quarterback for the Buckeyes. He even played basketball for the Buckeyes for a short time. Schlichter was the last starting quarterback for legendary Buckeyes coach Woody Hayes.

It was Schlichter who threw the interception in the 1978 Gator Bowl against Clemson. Tigers linebacker Charlie Bauman intercepted Schlichter's pass late in the game, and during Bauman's return, he was forced out of bounds on the Buckeyes' sideline. That's when Hayes threw the infamous punch at Bauman that eventually led to the coach's dismissal from Ohio State.

In three of Schlichter's four years with the Buckeyes, he finished in the top 10 in Heisman balloting. In 1979, the Buckeyes came closest to winning the national championship with Schlichter, but ultimately lost 17–16 to USC in the Rose Bowl.

After showing he was one of the best college players in the country, it appeared that Schlichter was headed for a successful career in the NFL. The Baltimore Colts picked him as the No. 4 overall pick in the 1982 draft, the same class that included BYU quarterback Jim McMahon and USC running back Marcus Allen. Unfortunately, Schlichter's short-lived and disappointing professional career was marred by his well-documented gambling troubles, which traced back to his collegiate days.

> **A**rt has all the basic ingredients for a great quarterback.
>
> —EARLE BRUCE

Art Schlichter's collegiate performance vaulted him to the NFL, but he would later find trouble off the field.

But even after Ohio State's touchdown, UCLA still had a chance. Ohio State's defense registered a sack and after two incomplete passes by quarterback Rick Bashore, the Bruins had the ball on fourth-and-19. UCLA picked up the first down when Bashore hit tight end Tim Wrightman on a 32-yard pass that took UCLA down to Ohio State's 46. Twelve seconds remained. After a Bruins timeout, their last, stopped the clock, the only thing UCLA could do on the next play was get the ball into the end zone. Buckeyes defensive back Mike Guess intercepted Bashore's pass at the 1-yard line, but even then, Ohio State wasn't out of the woods. The Buckeyes needed to run a play with one second left at their own 1, and in the game of football, crazy things can happen.

But not this time, and not with Schlichter, who was 13-of-22 for 159 yards, under center. He took the snap and pushed ahead into the line of scrimmage as the clock expired. And at that moment, Bruce was whisked away on the shoulders of his players as they celebrated a memorable win in Los Angeles.

Game Details

Ohio State 17 • UCLA 13

Ohio State	0	7	3	7	**17**
UCLA	10	0	0	3	**13**

Date: September 29, 1979
Team Records: Ohio State 4–0, UCLA 2–2
Scoring Plays:
UCLA—Curran 10-yard pass from Bashore (Boermeester PAT)
UCLA—Boermeester 27-yard FG
OSU—Murray 34-yard run (Janakievski PAT)
OSU—Janakievski 24-yard FG
UCLA—Boermeester 39-yard FG
OSU—Campbell 2-yard pass from Schlichter (Janakievski PAT)

January 1, 1997

Kissed By a Rose

Quarterback Joe Germaine Leads Buckeyes to Last-Second Win in Rose Bowl

You wouldn't have guessed it by the way he was nervously biting his fingernails, but Ohio State coach John Cooper never worried about his team coming back to defeat previously undefeated and untied Arizona State 20–17 in the 1997 Rose Bowl.

"I absolutely thought we had a chance to win it," Cooper said.

Just before Ohio State's game-winning touchdown, Arizona State quarterback Jake "the Snake" Plummer slithered his way into the end zone for an 11-yard touchdown run on third-and-11 that gave the Sun Devils a 17–14 lead with 1:40 left.

On the play, Buckeyes linebacker Andy Katzenmoyer had a hand on Plummer in the backfield. Katzenmoyer blitzed right through the middle of the line, but Plummer was able to slip away and scramble to the right. He then eluded a few more tackles, cut to the left, and dove across the goal line and into the end zone.

The touchdown prompted ABC announcer Dick Vermeil to say, "If I was John Cooper right now, I would be almost ready to die."

Ohio State quarterback Joe Germaine, however, wasn't worried.

"It was a tough feeling to see them go ahead like that late in the game," said Germaine, who orchestrated the Buckeyes' game-winning drive. "But we had confidence in ourselves that we could come back, make the plays, and win the game."

Germaine didn't start for Ohio State in the game, but that didn't bother him one bit. "The bottom line in any team sport is to win, no matter who plays," Germaine said. Stanley Jackson started for the Buckeyes and had helped Ohio State take a 7–0 lead in the first quarter with a touchdown pass to freshman David Boston.

But as Germaine said, it didn't matter who started. What mattered most was that he finished the game. And what a finish it was for Germaine, who hit Boston with the game-winning 5-yard touchdown pass with just 19 seconds remaining. Germaine's numbers weren't staggering (9-of-17 for 131 yards and two touchdowns) but he proved to be the best on the field when it counted—and he delivered in the clutch. That clutch performance also included a 72-yard touchdown pass to Dimitrious Stanley, good for a record for the longest touchdown reception in OSU bowl history.

I never saw him panic.
—JOHN COOPER

Wide receiver David Boston catches the game-winning touchdown in the 83rd Rose Bowl. *Photo courtesy of AP Images*

"We had a post-corner route, where David Boston was going to the inside then he was going to break it off and go back to the corner of the end zone," Cooper said about Boston's game-winning catch. Cooper said when he saw the defensive alignment and watched the play develop, he noticed that the defender on Boston stepped up to take the slant away, which put the defender in a bad position.

"At that moment, I thought we had a really good chance of being successful," Cooper said. "We had Joe Germaine throwing it and he was hot on that last drive. I mean, he had taken us right down the field. Then, of course, you had David Boston catching that touchdown pass."

Cooper said he recalled that the Arizona State defender fell down when Boston made that move to the inside and all Boston had to do was break to the corner of the end zone.

"I was elated after I saw David catch the ball," Cooper said. "That pass was like stealing candy from a baby. David

Quarterback Joe Germaine and head coach John Cooper hoist the Rose Bowl trophy in celebration of the Buckeyes' 20–17 victory over the Sun Devils. *Photo courtesy of AP Images*

Not Your Average Joe

Joe Germaine was named the Most Valuable Player of the Game in the 1997 Rose Bowl, but to Ohio State coach John Cooper, Germaine was his MVP long before.

"First of all, he was very accurate, he had a great work ethic, he was a very smart and intelligent quarterback, and he understood the offense," Cooper said. "And talk about a guy that was cool in the pocket. I have never seen a quarterback in college or the pros stay in the pocket and hold the ball as long as he did before he got rid of it.

"Now, sometimes that worked against him," Cooper said. "He would take a sack or get hit just as he released the ball. That happened a lot when he played for us and it happened a lot to him in the National Football League, but he was very, very cool;

very, very accurate; and very, very poised. Nothing rattled him...I never saw him panic."

Ohio State finished the season ranked No. 2 in the final polls after the Arizona State victory. The win prevented the Sun Devils, ranked No. 2 heading into the game, from at least sharing the national championship with No. 3 Florida, who had defeated No. 1 Florida State 52–20 in the Sugar Bowl.

Several players on the field that day went on to play in the NFL, including the late Pat Tillman along with Jake Plummer, Steve Bush, Derrick Rodgers, Jason Simmons, and Derek Smith of ASU and standouts Joe Germaine, Rob Kelly, Damon Moore, Orlando Pace, Shawn Springs, Mike Vrabel, and Antoine Winfield for the Buckeyes.

was wide open in the corner and that had to be the easiest throw for Joe the whole drive."

Cooper said the win was special in so many ways, mainly because critics started to question whether Cooper and Ohio State could win the "big game." It was also special because Cooper made history.

"That game was special for me because I became the only coach in the history of college football to win the Rose Bowl as the head coach from a Pac-10 conference school in 1987 (with Arizona State) and from a Big Ten school 10 years later."

After the game, linebacker Matt Wilhelm told a television reporter on the field, "It's awesome. To come back and perform the way we did, it was a great victory for us."

Running back Pepe Pearson, said, "This is the most exciting moment of my life. The Rose Bowl...it's like the Super Bowl."

Then, defensive lineman Luke Fickell said, "I don't think I can describe this any other way. If I write a book some day, this is exactly how I would write it."

Game Details

Ohio State 20 • Arizona State 17

Arizona State	0	7	3	7	**17**
Ohio State	7	0	7	6	**20**

Date: January 1, 1997

Team Records: Ohio State 11–1, Arizona State 11–1

Scoring Plays:

OSU—Boston 9-yard pass from S. Jackson (J. Jackson PAT)

ASU—Boyer 25-yard pass from Plummer (Nycz PAT)

ASU—Nycz 37-yard FG

OSU—Stanley 72-yard pass from Germaine (J. Jackson PAT)

ASU—Plummer 11-yard run (Nycz kick)

OSU—Boston 5-yard pass from Germaine (PAT failed)

January 2, 2006

Fiesta! Fiesta!

Ohio State Wide Receiver Santonio Holmes Sets Bowl Record with Catch

His speed was unbelievably impressive. And his receiving skills matched his speed.

That's why Ohio State wide receiver Santonio Holmes was such an impact player throughout his career with the Buckeyes. That explosiveness was on display in the 2006 Fiesta Bowl, when Ohio State dominated quarterback Brady Quinn and the Notre Dame Fighting Irish 34–20.

As a senior, Holmes set a Fiesta Bowl record with his 85-yard touchdown catch from quarterback Troy Smith just before halftime. The longest-ever in bowl history, the score gave Ohio State a 21–7 halftime lead. Coach Tressel said that the game plan was to try to spread the ball against the Irish using wide receiver Ted Ginn Jr. and Holmes.

"That was a huge part of our game plan," Tressel said. "[Offensive coordinator Jim] Bollman and his staff worked long and hard for a month, watching where we thought we could make some big things happen, and I thought they had a tremendous plan, and our guys executed it so well. The one thing we talked about is, we didn't want to overthrow the deep ones. We didn't want to misthrow them or ovethrow them."

Holmes' catch was a combination of several perfect executions. First, Smith executed a perfect play-action fake, holding Notre Dame's linebackers and secondary momentarily. Second, Holmes was split

Santonio Holmes makes a move
against two Irish defenders.

wide right and with his blazing speed, he raced straight down the field and was able to get behind Notre Dame's entire secondary. Finally, the offensive line provided excellent protection to Smith. Smith tossed a perfect strike, hitting Holmes in stride at Notre Dame's 45. From there, it was off to the races, as Holmes outran the Irish defenders into the end zone.

"Santonio means a lot to the whole offense, and for me as a quarterback, he takes a lot of burdens and situations off my shoulder, because he's a student of the game as well," Smith said. "He understands and sees things just the way I do. From day one, he's been a great receiver, he's been a great guy, a team leader. And like the coach said, it's time for him to step up and go to another level. He's done pretty much everything we've asked of him here."

The Buckeyes' game plan for spreading things out and opening the Irish up was firing on all cylinders. Previous to Holmes' touchdown, Ginn Jr. had already scored two of his own, on a 56-yard touchdown pass from Smith and on a 68-yard reverse just minutes later.

"I had a lot of fun," Ginn said. "The point of the whole game was to play hard for the seniors. I have another year and the seniors don't. I try to go out and play hard and play fast and do everything right."

Smith added, "The scheme was we set out to make big plays…we really, really set out this week to not overthrow the deep ball. The guys stepped up today, and the offensive line did a great job with withstanding the blitzes that came, and I was fortunate to be able to connect on a couple deep passes."

With the win, Tressel had won four bowl games in his first five years at Ohio State.

"Well, the secret to the success is [linebacker] A.J. Hawk, Troy and Teddy, and [former players] Will Smith and Craig Krenzel, and all the rest," Tressel said. "We have a great coaching staff and great players. Why we have been so blessed to be here at the Fiesta Bowl, you have no idea. It's the most wonderful bowl you can possibly be a part of it. We've enjoyed every minute of it. The people here are

> **I**t's time for him to step up and go to another level.
>
> —TROY SMITH

Game Details

Ohio State 34 • Notre Dame 20

Ohio State	7	14	3	10	**34**
Notre Dame	7	0	6	7	**20**

Date: January 2, 2006

Team Records: Ohio State 10–2, Notre Dame 9–3

Scoring Plays:

ND—Walker 20-yard run (Fitzpatrick PAT)

OSU—Ginn Jr. 56-yard pass from Smith (Huston PAT)

OSU—Ginn Jr. 68-yard run (Huston PAT)

OSU—Holmes 85-yard pass from Smith (Huston PAT)

ND—Walker 10-yard run (kick failed)

OSU—Huston 40-yard FG

OSU—Huston 26-yard FG

ND—Walker 3-yard run (Fitzpatrick PAT)

OSU—Pittman 60-yard run (Huston PAT)

extraordinary, and anyone that gets an opportunity to play in the Fiesta Bowl is fortunate."

Hawk said, "I think you have to give a lot of credit to the coaches. I was thinking about what everyone was saying about giving [Notre Dame] Coach [Charlie] Weis four weeks to prepare. What about giving Coach Tressel four weeks to prepare for you? He's four out of five in the bowl games. That's where I think the focus should have been from you guys. I think our coach did a great job finding the perfect balance."

Santonio Holmes

When Buckeyes wide receiver Santonio Holmes left Ohio State to enter the NFL draft, he still had a year of eligibility remaining. (He was redshirted in 2002, the year the Buckeyes won the national championship.) During his career with the Buckeyes, Holmes caught 240 passes for 3,496 yards, the fifth highest in school history and third in touchdowns with 25 at the time of his departure.

Coach Tressel shared this advice for Holmes, who really wanted to leave for the NFL and forego his last year of eligibility.

"Santonio talked about it many times," Tressel said. "I've even inferred it quite often, as I've talked publicly. He's a fourth-year guy and well along toward his degree. I think it's the right time for him to go.

I think he's proven it. In my mind, I don't know how many guys would be drafted ahead of him. He's a playmaker, blocker, return man. And I always tell my guys, 'If you're going to be in the first round, you probably need to go,' and Santonio is going to be in the first round."

Tressel was right. Holmes was the 25th overall pick in the 2006 NFL Draft by the Pittsburgh Steelers. A few years later in Super Bowl XLIII, Holmes made the game-winning catch with 35 seconds left to help the Steelers defeat the Arizona Cardinals. Holmes finished with nine catches for 131 yards and a touchdown, had four catches from quarterback Ben Roethlisberger on the Steelers' game-winning drive, and was named Super Bowl MVP.

Holmes made plenty of unforgettable catches during his days at OSU (like this one against Michigan in 2004), but he is best known for his tiptoed touchdown catch in Super Bowl XLIII with the Pittsburgh Steelers.

Michael Jenkins hauls in the game-winning touchdown pass over Boilermakers cornerback Antwaun Rogers.

November 9, 2002

Going For It All

With the Game on the Line, Krenzel Decides to Go
Deep Against Purdue

On fourth down and late in the fourth quarter, Ohio State
trailed the Purdue Boilermakers by three points. The hopes
of playing for a national championship looked slim. All the
Buckeyes needed was just one yard. And with Coach Jim
Tressel at the helm, almost all of the 65,250 fans at Ross-Ade
Stadium in West Lafayette, Indiana, including the Ohio State
fans, just knew that the Buckeyes would try to run the ball for
the first down.

But as the television character Gomer Pyle routinely exclaimed, "Surprise,
surprise, surprise!"

And boy, were the Boilermakers and their fans surprised when Ohio State
quarterback Craig Krenzel hit wide receiver Michael Jenkins on a 37-yard
touchdown pass with just 1:36 left in the game. That score gave the Buckeyes
yet another come-from-behind win that season.

However, before Jenkins' catch, Ohio State was facing a third-and-14 situation right at midfield with 2:26 left. Krenzel took the snap out of the shotgun
and stepped up in the pocket to avoid pressure. Just before he was hit, he
found tight end Ben Hartsock wide open at the Purdue 40. Hartsock lunged
forward, trying to get to the first-down marker but fell a yard short.

"Now, you're so close, you have to go [for it]," ABC television announcer
Brent Musburger said. "And you can run for it if you want to."

Musburger was right on one account: Tressel did go for it. But it wasn't a run play at all, as Jenkins made the catch in the left corner of the end zone with Purdue defensive back Antwaun Rogers in tight coverage. The Ohio State fans watching and listening to the game on ABC's nationally televised broadcast heard Musburger utter the words, "Holy Buckeye." That famed line resonated with so many Ohio State fans who couldn't believe that the Buckeyes pulled out yet another last-minute win, keeping their beloved team undefeated with two games remaining in the regular season.

Ohio State was trailing 6–3 late in the game, and up to that point the Big Ten contest was a defensive battle with all of the offense coming on field goals: two by Purdue's

Ohio State prevailed against Purdue on the strength of quarterback Craig Krenzel's arm—and legs.

Berlin Lacevic (21 and 32 yards, respectively) and a 22-yard field goal by Ohio State's Mike Nugent. And before Jenkins' game-winning catch from Krenzel, Tressel could have opted for a 54-yard field goal attempt by Nugent to tie the game. Knowing Tressel's conservative track record, the kick seemed like the most logical strategy. Instead, Tressel went with what Krenzel was feeling.

For the record, the play was called "King Right 64 Y Shallow Swap."

"Michael Jenkins ran a go route and I'm pretty sure coach Tressel was probably surprised I threw the ball there," Krenzel said. "There were a number of underneath options that were more short to intermediate routes that we were really looking to call to just get the first down."

Still, Tressel not opting to run one yard for the first down and actually throw the ball on fourth-and-1 was a shock. But not for Krenzel.

"The defensive look that [Purdue] gave us, I knew what they were trying to do," Krenzel said. "Our guys up front protected well and I knew I had Michael one-on-one on the outside. Regardless of the situation, that's a matchup that you just can't pass up."

Game Details

Ohio State 10 • Purdue 6

Ohio State	0	3	0	7	**10**
Purdue	3	0	0	3	**6**

Date: November 9, 2002
Team Records: Ohio State 11–0, Purdue (4–6)
Scoring Plays:
PU— Lacevic 21-yard FG
OSU—Mike Nugent 22-yard FG
PU—Lacevic 32-yard FG
OSU—Jenkins 37-yard pass from Krenzel (Nugent PAT)

Fortunate, but Not Lucky

Michael Jenkins' game-winning touchdown catch against Purdue was his fifth catch of the afternoon. He finished the day with 87 yards receiving, and he also contributed in a big way on special teams with a blocked punt late in the third quarter.

With a game that could have very easily gone the other way for the Buckeyes, Coach Tressel felt fortunate, but not necessarily lucky.

"We kept hanging in there, plugging away," Tressel said. "And we always talk about the fact that if we keep banging, something good is going to happen."

Craig Krenzel was 13-of-20 for 173 yards, 37 of those passing yards in the last minute that decided the game.

"Purdue's defense seemed to think that we were running," Krenzel said about the touchdown pass to Jenkins. "I would probably think that on fourth-and-1. I was throwing into the wind. Fortunately our offense stepped up, I stepped into the pass, and it floated over his shoulder."

Ohio State's defense played well too, holding Purdue to just 56 yards on 29 carries. The Boilermakers' leading rusher was Brandon Jones, who carried the ball 12 times for just 28 yards. The Buckeyes' defense, led by cornerback Chris Gamble, who picked off Purdue quarterback Kyle Orton to preserve the win, and middle linebacker Matt Wilhelm, who also had an interception in the game, helped give Krenzel and Jenkins their chance to be heroes on the afternoon.

That's a matchup that you just can't pass up.
—CRAIG KRENZEL

Bobby Olive didn't have to wait long to show the LSU Tigers the talent they passed up.

September 24, 1988

Olive's Coming-Out Party

Wide Receiver Bobby Olive Shows LSU What Could've Been

As far as Atlanta native Bobby Olive was concerned, there was no trace of revenge on his mind. He wasn't bitter, either, that a southern school like LSU recruited him but *didn't* want to offer him a scholarship. Olive knew in his heart he was a major Division I player who could earn a scholarship somewhere, even if it wasn't at LSU.

So Olive chose to play at Ohio State, another school that *didn't* offer him a scholarship.

"I had to walk on at Ohio State," Olive said proudly.

Yes, proudly, because Olive knew he was going to prove himself. That opportunity came a lot quicker than he imagined, early in his first season. It came against LSU, a team that was undefeated, ranked No. 7 in the country, and had clobbered Texas A&M and Tennessee by a combined score of 61–9. The unranked and youthful Buckeyes, under first-year coach John Cooper, seemingly had no chance.

"We were not a very good football team at that stage of the season," Cooper said. "That was my first year. It was one of our big, big upsets because LSU had beaten Tennessee the week before."

None of that mattered to Olive and the Buckeyes—at least in the final five minutes. LSU was leading 33–20 in the final quarter at the Shoe. "We needed to score some touchdowns but we also needed some stops on defense," Olive said. "But more than anything, what I remember most about that fourth quarter is that we seated about 95,000 people in the stadium at the time, but we were down by two touchdowns. I guarantee you, when we were down two touchdowns with about five minutes left there probably were only around 45,000 people there. People left the stadium because they thought it was over."

Those people who left didn't get a chance to witness one of the most memorable comebacks *and* game-winning catches at the Shoe.

It started with a five-yard touchdown run by Carlos Snow that cut the LSU lead to 33–27. The Buckeyes added two more points on an intentional safety by LSU, and with less than two minutes left, the Buckeyes trailed just 33–29.

On the free kick, Olive did some nifty running and returned the ball to LSU's 39, giving the Buckeyes excellent field position with 1:24 left. This was Olive's dream: to be in a position to beat LSU. And the dream became a reality when Ohio State quarterback Greg Frey hit Olive on a 20-yard touchdown catch—an outstanding diving catch in the end zone—with 38 seconds remaining that put the Buckeyes ahead 38–33 and sent the remaining Buckeyes fans in a frenzied celebration.

An amusing note is that Olive was trying to do the then-popular "cabbage patch" dance in the end zone, but as soon as he started to bust his move, he was mobbed by his teammates.

"We knew LSU was playing man-to-man coverage, so it was basically pick your poison," Olive said about the play. "Whichever defensive back we felt we could complete the post route on, that's the one we attacked.

"The biggest thing that I remember about that catch was, first, that was Coach Cooper's first year and he was still trying to win over the Buckeye Nation," Olive said. "Cooper was coming off a Rose Bowl win as the head coach of Arizona State. So for him to have such a big win

The Ohio State drum major pumps up the crowd.

Game Details

Ohio State 36 • LSU 33

LSU	3	10	10	10	**33**
Ohio State	0	14	3	19	**36**

Date: September 24, 1988

Team Records: Ohio State 2–1, LSU 2–1

Scoring Plays:

LSU—Browndyke 36-yard FG

OSU—Snow 1-yard run (O'Morrow PAT)

OSU—McCray 23-yard blocked punt return (O'Morrow PAT)

LSU—Moss 30-yard pass from Hodson (Browndyke PAT)

LSU—Browndyke 27-yard FG

OSU—O'Morrow 35-yard FG

LSU—E. Fuller 4-yard run (Browndyke PAT)

LSU—Browndyke 35-yard FG

OSU—O'Morrow 41-yard FG

LSU—Browndyke 20-yard FG

LSU—Lee 55-yard pass from Hodson (Browndyke PAT)

OSU—Snow 5-yard run (O'Morrow PAT)

OSU—Bourgeois ran out of end zone/safety

OSU—Olive 20-yard pass from Frey (O'Morrow PAT)

so early in the season and in his coaching career at Ohio State was big, really big."

Cooper said he was proud of Olive and the rest of the team for stepping up and showing what they were made of and against such a strong opponent. He respected that about his players.

"We faced an outstanding football team, and that was a game we had no reason winning, *at all*," Cooper said. "It was a great, great comeback. The touchdown pass was a post route, and Greg put it right where it had to be. If he didn't, we would've lost. And if Bobby didn't catch it, we would've lost. Again, it was a great, great comeback and Bobby Olive showed he was a clutch receiver."

Olive, meanwhile, felt he had arrived and Columbus was going to love him, which it did.

"As a sophomore, that was my first time really playing in a big college game on national television. It

was my first collegiate touchdown. A lot happened [in] that game," he recalled.

Olive said that play, that catch, that come-from-behind victory all changed his collegiate career.

"The way I came to Ohio State, I had to walk on," Olive said, again with pride. "But not only did that catch prove to me that I could play big-time Division I college football, it showed that I could actually be a playmaker. So it was like a coming-out party for me. And it was even sweeter because LSU didn't offer me a scholarship. It was sweet for me to have such a big game against LSU on such a big stage."

The Last-Second Catch

It's one thing to find yourself trailing at home, but it's even more demoralizing when you're trying to fight back and your opponent scores on a fluke.

But that was exactly the situation the Buckeyes and first-year coach John Cooper found themselves in. LSU entered the game undefeated and ranked No. 6 in the country. The Tigers had won 14 straight road games led by quarterback Tommy Hodson. But it didn't matter to Ohio State as the Buckeyes played right with LSU.

But with 4:29 left, the Tigers scored on a deflection that resulted in a 55-yard touchdown reception for a 33–20 lead. As one television announcer said after the touchdown, "The score is certainly not indicative of how tight this game has been."

He was right.

There's a good reason why the Buckeyes didn't give up and didn't panic. They fought back and gave themselves a chance to win. And with two players like wide receiver Bobby Olive and quarterback Greg Frey on offense, Ohio State fans liked their chances.

"What that win did for us was really big," Cooper said. "The one thing we did when I came here was we expanded the recruiting base. We started going nationwide with recruiting. To beat an LSU [team] that was ranked in the Top 10 in the country and playing them on national television, I think that really helped us with our recruiting the next year. We started going nationwide. We went out to Houston and got [wide receiver] David Boston, we went to Arizona and got [quarterback] Joe Germaine. We did a lot of out-of-state recruiting in the next few years after that win. That game really showed the nation what kind of football we were going to play and we were going to be wide open. We were going to throw it, we were going to take chances."

November 17, 1984

A Chance at Redemption

Wide Receiver Mike Lanese Makes Up For Early Fumble with Big Third-Down Catch

A 17-yard catch in a 21–6 game wouldn't seem like a big deal under normal circumstances. But Lanese's catch at home against Michigan in 1984 was indeed a big deal. Not only was the game much closer than the final score would indicate, but also the Big Ten championship was on the line.

In fact, it was such a big catch that Lanese wrote a chapter about it for the book *Game of My Life: Memorable Stories of Ohio State Football*, written by his wife, Laura Lanese, and Steve Greenberg.

Throughout the history of the Ohio State–Michigan rivalry, educated and civilized commentators on both sides have often waxed poetic about the deep, enduring respect and admiration they had for each other's program. For me, not so much. Call me a cad for saying so, but I've really never cared much for anything that's come out of Michigan. Despite nearly committing to Bo Schembechler as a 17 year-old recruit,

I'm pretty certain I've never liked Michigan. Even growing up in the Wolverine-friendly Cleveland area, I knew I didn't like Michigan before I'd even watched my first college football game. In fact, looking back, I can't remember ever not feeling anything but contempt for Michigan, including their players, their school, their fans and their song. Especially their song.

That was just the way it was for Lanese and his feelings toward Michigan. And so, when he fumbled on a punt return that ultimately led to a field goal for Michigan, you could understand his feelings. "Naturally, my only thought at that point, like any sane player in that situation, was to sneak back to the sideline without giving [Coach] Earle [Bruce] a chance to grab me," Lanese said. "That plan failed as well. Years later—I forget the exact phrase Earle used when he caught up to me—but I'm pretty sure I could figure it out without buying any vowels."

Mike Lanese stretches out for a catch against Michigan. *Photo courtesy of Ohio State University Photo Archives*

Ohio State still led 7–3 after Lanese's fumble and Michigan's subsequent field goal. "All I wanted was another shot at a big play…one play that could shift the game's momentum," Lanese said. "You can never undo a bad decision. But there are two halves in football, each offering opportunities for success, and, I suppose, failure. But who thinks about failure in the middle of a Michigan game?"

Ohio State led 7–6 midway through the fourth quarter and started to move the ball using tight end Eddie Taggart.

Then the Buckeyes were faced with a third-and-12 situation at their own 43. Quarterback Mike Tomczak dropped back to pass, desperately needing a first down and a score to take control of the game—and the season.

Lanese was just at the first-down marker, at the Michigan 48, but there were three defenders in the area too. Miraculously, Lanese contorted his body like Harry Houdini, left his feet, and made a diving catch with both hands for the first down.

Mike Lanese hangs tough. *Photo courtesy of Ohio State University Photo Archives*

Mike Lanese

Mike Lanese epitomized the term student-athlete, as he exemplified both during his career at Ohio State. A two-time Academic All-American, during his senior season in 1985, Lanese was also cocaptain that year. A year later, he was one of 32 Rhodes Scholars and spent two years at Worcester College in Oxford studying philosophy, politics, and economics. After returning to the United States, he became an officer in the U.S. Navy. Once he graduated from Officer Candidate School, he served onboard *USS Sterett* (CG-31) as a Surface Warfare Officer from 1989 to 1993.

After the Navy, Lanese had a brief stint with the Cleveland Browns in 1988 as a free agent. Some of his OSU teammates went on to have impressive NFL careers.

In an interview, Lanese once said, "Not many teams have a legitimate chance to win a national championship. Some guys never play for a team with a shot. We had more talent in 1984 than in any other year of my career. Guys like Keith Byars, Pepper Johnson, Cris Carter, Jim Lachey. All that talent and we just couldn't pull it together. Maybe it just wasn't meant to be, or the stars weren't aligned properly, or the football gods simply deemed us unworthy. There are thousands of things we could have done differently, and the what-ifs can drive you crazy."

"As it turned out, because I caught the ball, we kept a drive alive and the momentum seemed to change," Lanese said. "We scored a few plays later, and then again late in the quarter before running out the clock. We won the game 21–6, locking up the Big Ten championship and securing a berth in the 1985 Rose Bowl. As a result of the catch, I was named the Chevrolet Most Valuable Player of the Game. Of the *Michigan* game.

"I'm not an expert on the subject, but I'd guess that part of creating a memorable moment is not realizing at the time you're creating one," Lanese said. "Ordinary often becomes remarkable not by intent but by circumstance and perception. The play would later be seen as pivotal in the outcome of the game. I've made better catches. But not on that stage and not in that moment and not in that context. Had we not scored on that possession, the catch would have been entirely forgettable, tucked away quietly into the big book of OSU football statistics as just another 17-yard reception."

> **W**ho thinks about failure in the middle of a Michigan game?
>
> —MIKE LANESE

Game Details

Ohio State 21 • Michigan 6

Michigan	0	3	3	0	**6**
Ohio State	7	0	0	14	**21**

Date: November 17, 1984

Team Records: Ohio State 9-2, Michigan 6-5

Scoring Plays:

OSU—Byars 1-yard run (Spangler kick)

UM—Bergeron 37-yard FG

UM—Bergeron 45-yard FG

OSU—Byars 2-yard run (Spangler kick)

OSU—Byars 2-yard run (Spangler kick)

Unbelievable Runs

September 30, 1972

The Archie Griffin Era Begins

Freshman Running Back Dazzles and Amazes the Crowd at Ohio Stadium with an Unbelievable Performance

Columbus native Archie Griffin, college football's only two-time Heisman Trophy winner, was probably one of the most humble and caring players to ever play for the Buckeyes. Consider this gesture, which he made during his senior season in 1972.

Griffin had already won the Heisman Trophy the previous year as a junior and was about to make history by winning it a second time. But Griffin wasn't even named the *team* MVP his senior year. That honor and distinction went to quarterback Cornelius Greene, who deserved the award as much as Griffin. In fact, in a team vote that was close, it was Griffin who cast the deciding vote, naming Greene as the team MVP.

Coach Woody Hayes described Griffin as "a better young man than he is a football

player, and he's the best football player I've ever seen."

Well, what Ohio State fans saw during Griffin's freshman season was sheer greatness in the making. In his second collegiate game, with the Buckeyes hosting North Carolina, Griffin said he wasn't expecting to play. In the previous game, a 21–0 win against Iowa in the season opener, Griffin had a fumble—a fact that hadn't sat well with Hayes. The Buckeyes had a week off before hosting North Carolina, and Griffin had dropped on the depth chart.

But eventually Griffin got the call. "Griffin, get in there," Hayes was reported as saying.

Was Griffin surprised?

Absolutely.

"My fondest memory playing in Ohio Stadium would have to be September 30, 1972," Griffin said. "I was a freshman, and that was the first year that freshmen were

I had no idea that I was going to get onto the football field.

—ARCHIE GRIFFIN

Running back Archie Griffin remains the only athlete to have won the Heisman Trophy twice. *Photo courtesy of AP Images*

THE HEISMAN MEMORIAL TROPHY
AWARDED ANNUALLY TO THE OUTSTANDING COLLEGE FOOTBALL PLAYER IN THE
UNITED STATES BY THE DOWNTOWN ATHLETIC CLUB OF NEW YORK CITY, INC.
WINNERS TO DATE

1971 - PAT SULLIVAN, AUBURN UNIVERSITY
1972 - JOHNNY RODGERS, UNIVERSITY OF NEBRASKA
1973 - JOHN CAPPELLETTI, PENNSYLVANIA STATE UNIVERSITY

The Heisman Kid

All you needed to do was hear Archie Griffin's emotional Heisman Trophy acceptance speech in 1974, when he won the prestigious award as a junior, to understand the type of man Griffin was and what The Ohio State University meant to him. Griffin handily beat out USC senior running back Anthony Davis in the balloting with 1,920 points. Davis finished with 819.

"The way it is with me," Griffin said, stopping in between words as he was overcome with emotion, "especially after the announcement last week that I had won. I couldn't believe it, and I'm not sure now that I do."

Then in December 2009 on CBSSports.com with Jason Horowitz, Griffin appeared to talk about Florida quarterback Tim Tebow. Tebow had already won the Heisman Trophy in 2007 and had a chance to become just the second player in college football history to win the award twice in a career. Tebow ultimately lost the Heisman to Alabama running back Mack Ingram.

Horowitz asked Griffin—who amassed 5,589 career yards, and 100 or more yards in an NCAA-record 31 consecutive games—what that honor was like. Griffin gave yet another classy answer.

"Just winning one Heisman Trophy means a great deal," Griffin told Horowitz. "And to have done it twice, it makes it extra special because at the time, I didn't know that they'd even give it to anybody twice. And to have that award, I'm very proud of it. I'm very proud of it because it speaks for the teams that I've played on during my time at Ohio State. I've been very fortunate to have been in the right place at the right time with the right people and that's what made it happen, my teammates, my coaches and all of that. It fell just right and I'm sure appreciative of it."

Griffin was a key player in Buckeyes football during the Hayes era. *Photo courtesy of Ohio State University Photo Archives*

eligible to play varsity football. I got in the game and we were down 7–0 and I had no idea that I was going to get onto the football field."

Griffin got in the game and quickly showed that he had the potential to be one of the greatest running backs in Ohio State history in just one fall afternoon. That's how special of a player he was. He rushed for 239 yards, which at that time was an Ohio State rushing record; 111 of them in the first half, on just 16 carries.

The Buckeyes went on to defeat North Carolina 29–14, and Griffin established himself as the Ohio State running back of the future. He also went on to lead the Buckeyes in rushing his freshman year, with 867 yards.

"That was the most exciting moment I had in all of football, if you really want to know the truth," Griffin said. "I've played in four Rose Bowls, four Michigan games, and even the Super Bowl, but that was the most exciting moment because I had no idea that I'd get in that game. It was a total surprise for me, and I count it as a miracle."

Game Details

Ohio State 29 • North Carolina 14

North Carolina	7	0	0	7	**14**
Ohio State	3	6	14	6	**29**

Date: September 30, 1972

Team Records: Ohio State 2–0, North Carolina 3–1

Scoring Plays:

UNC—Brown recovered blocked punt in end zone (Alexander PAT)

OSU—Conway 22-yard FG

OSU—Hare 17-yard run (PAT failed)

OSU—Keith 11-yard run (Conway PAT)

OSU—Henson 1-yard run (Conway PAT)

OSU—Griffin 9-yard run (PAT failed)

UNC—Bathea 37-yard pass from Vidnovic (Alexander PAT)

Beanie Wells barrels his way over Michigan defenders on his way into the end zone. *Photo courtesy of AP Images*

Run, Beanie, Run!

Chris "Beanie" Wells Scores on a 52-Yard Run That Ushered In the Buckeyes' "Beanie Era"

Over the years, there have been many great running backs who have laced up their cleats for the Buckeyes, and countless touchdown runs labeled "spectacular" or "legendary." Inarguably, Chris "Beanie" Wells' 52-yard touchdown run in a 42–39 win against Michigan in 2006 was one of those runs.

Wells was the No. 1 running back recruit in the country, coming out of Akron Garfield High School—the same school that produced former OSU All-American cornerback Antoine Winfield, and the same city that produced former All–Big Ten OSU running back Antonio Pittman and All–Big Ten Northwestern running back Tyrell Sutton. Akron has another famous homegrown athlete too: LeBron James, who was a first-team All-State wide receiver during his days at St. Vincent-St. Mary High School.

As for Wells' touchdown run, it was, to borrow a phrase from Steely Dan, "perfection and grace." It was beauty and brawn. It was speed and agility and much, much more. And when it was over, it was an instant classic.

The Buckeyes entered the game undefeated and ranked No. 1 in the country. Michigan was ranked No. 2 and also was undefeated. The Wolverines jumped out to an early 7–0 lead after a 1-yard touchdown run by Michigan running back Michael Hart and an extra point just two-and-a-half minutes into the game.

Ohio State tied the score four minutes later on a 1-yard touchdown pass from Troy Smith to wide receiver Roy Hall and that was the score at the end of the first quarter.

Then Wells electrified the crowd of 105,708 fans in the Shoe. As the lone running back, he took the handoff from Smith and started to run left. But almost immediately after the snap, a Michigan defender slipped through the line of scrimmage and seemed to be poised to take Beanie down for a loss.

It didn't happen.

Beanie came up with a perfectly executed spin move at the right moment to avoid the tackle-for-loss. From there, the play turned into an exhibition of Beanie's highly underrated speed for a big running back. He hit the line of scrimmage, threw out an incredible stiff-arm to avoid another would-be Michigan tackler, then turned on the jets and outraced everyone on the field into the end zone to give the Buckeyes a 14–7 lead, a lead they would never relinquish.

Naturally, Beanie's touchdown run was sensational, but what made it special was the fact that Ohio State fans were rooting for him and were in his corner all season. Earlier in the year, Beanie experienced problems with holding onto the ball. He had a severe case of "fumble-itis."

Early in the season, Tressel was asked if he had the confidence in Wells to use him in crucial situations, in light of his fumbling episodes.

Tressel didn't hesitate.

"Absolutely," Tressel said.

Beanie finished with 576 yards and seven touchdowns on 104 carries playing behind his hometown teammate, Pittman—impressive numbers for a backup freshman. Beanie did have to overcome that issue with the fumbles, but he said having to go through the adversity being sidelined on several occasions after fumbling made him a better player.

"No matter what obstacles that you might face on the field and in life, if you keep a positive attitude, you'll be more likely to get through those situations," Wells said. "That's what I learned my freshman year and that's why I kept myself ready at all times, especially for the Michigan game that year."

Ohio State pushed the lead to 35–24 midway through the third quarter on a 56-yard touchdown run by Pittman, which made the score 35–24. But Michigan fought back and cut the lead to 35–31, on a 1-yard run by Hart with 14:41 left in the game.

With 2:16 left to play, Michigan scored on a 16-yard touchdown pass from Chad Henne to Tyler Ecker. In fact, Michigan outscored Ohio State 25–14 in the second half. But the key to Ohio State's win was the fact that Beanie's 52-yard touchdown run helped the Buckeyes score 21 second-quarter points for a 28–14 edge—and it was that run that set the tone for the rest of the game. It let the Wolverines know that they were in for a battle, and that a freshman kid from Akron named Beanie—yes, *Beanie*—was leading the way.

Game Details

Ohio State 42 • Michigan 39

Michigan	7	7	10	15	**39**
Ohio State	7	21	7	7	**42**

Date: November 18, 2006

Team Records: Ohio State 12–0, Michigan 11–1

Scoring Plays:

UM—Hart 1-yard run (Rivas PAT)

OSU—Hall 1-yard pass from Smith (Pettrey PAT)

OSU—Wells 52-yard run (Pettrey PAT)

OSU—Ginn Jr. 39-yard pass from Smith (Pettrey PAT)

UM—Arrington 37-yard pass from Henne (Rivas PAT)

OSU—Gonzalez 8-yard pass from Smith (Pettrey PAT)

UM—Hart 2-yard run (Rivas PAT)

UM—Rivas 39-yard FG

OSU—Pittman 56-yard run (Pettrey PAT)

UM—Hart 1-yard run (Rivas PAT)

OSU—Robiskie 13-yard pass from Smith (Pettrey PAT)

UM—Ecker 16-yard pass from Henne (Breaston pass from Henne)

"Beanie"

The nickname "Beanie" was bestowed by his older brother, Ray Wells, who said when his younger brother, Chris, was a kid, he was so skinny he looked like a string bean. That's how the legend of Beanie Wells started.

Of course, Beanie grew into his big frame in time. And he went on to an outstanding collegiate career at Ohio State.

Naturally, the most avid Ohio State fan hopes that the Buckeyes will play for a national championship every year. If that doesn't happen, the next best thing is to beat Michigan every year. Ohio State players can make a name for themselves in Buckeyes lore with outstanding performances against the Wolverines. Beanie was incredible in his three games against Michigan, all of them wins.

During his freshman season, Beanie had 56 yards on five carries, including that stupendous 52-yard touchdown in the second quarter in a 42–39 win.

The following year, Beanie was magnificent in a 14–3 win in Ann Arbor. He finished with 222 yards on 39 carries and scored on a 62-yard touchdown run.

And during his junior year, he rushed for 134 yards on 15 carries and scored on a 59-yard touchdown run in the Buckeyes' 42–7 win in Columbus.

Beanie decided to forego his final year of college eligibility at Ohio State and was a first-round pick, the 31st pick overall, by the Arizona Cardinals in 2009, where he had a solid rookie season. He finished the season with 793 yards on 176 carries, averaging 4.5 yards a game, and scored seven touchdowns.

No matter what obstacles that you might face on the field and in life, if you keep a positive attitude, you'll be more likely to get through those situations.

—BEANIE WELLS

Chris "Beanie" Wells shows off his specialty: crossing the goal line.
Photo courtesy of AP Images

November 2, 1985

Amazing "Feet"

Wooldridge Doesn't Let Cracked Rib Stop Him from Stepping Up

Ohio State's 22–13 win against Iowa seemed improbable to most for several reasons. The Buckeyes were taking on the high-powered Hawkeyes in Columbus—without Ohio State preseason Heisman Trophy candidate and senior running back Keith Byars. He had battled a foot injury all season and wasn't healthy enough to play. In the previous year, Byars finished second in the Heisman balloting behind Doug Flutie of Boston College, so not having Byars in the mix was a huge disadvantage for the Buckeyes.

Sophomore running back Johnny Wooldridge had a cracked rib from the Minnesota game a week earlier and wasn't close to being 100 percent. In fact, he never even expected to see action against Iowa, which was ranked No. 1 in the country at the time. (The Buckeyes were ranked No. 8.)

Behind Wooldridge was freshman Vince Workman. So with Byars ailing, the running game was placed squarely on Wooldridge and Workman.

"We were kind of left with, 'Can John go? Will John go? How long will he be able to go?'" Wooldridge said. "And if not, we're going to have to rely on this fresh-man tailback in Workman. But ironically, against Minnesota the week before, after Keith got hurt and after I got hurt, Vince came in against Minnesota and had one of the final touchdowns to help us get the win in the Metrodome. So Vince had at least that much experience, if he had to go against Iowa."

Leading up to the Iowa game, Wooldridge had hardly practiced at all that week. He was wearing a rib protector—the kind that quarterbacks usually wear—and he

Running back John Wooldridge leaves the defenders in the dust. *Photo courtesy of Ohio State University Photo Archives*

couldn't move or breathe easily. When he did take a deep breath, he would cough up blood. By Friday, Wooldridge had barely taken a snap in practice.

Heading into the game, Coach Earle Bruce had to make a decision. "Coach Bruce said, 'John, we don't know if you're ready and we don't think you can go so we're going to start Vince,'" Wooldridge said. "I thought that was a good idea."

Iowa was led by quarterback Chuck Long, who was the leading candidate for the Heisman that season. For Ohio State to have any chance at beating the Hawkeyes, the Buckeyes needed to be healthy, and they weren't.

Veteran quarterback Jim Karsatos was effective in spreading the ball around to his outstanding receivers Cris Carter and Mike Lanese. And tight end Eddie Taggart

The Ohio State Buckeyes football team rallies around head coach Earle Bruce. *Photo courtesy of AP Images*

Byars Inspires

The night before the Iowa game, Ohio State running back Johnny Wooldridge said Keith Byars delivered a classic pregame meal speech that helped inspire the Buckeyes to their upset win at home against the previously No. 1–ranked Hawkeyes.

"Keith knew I was banged up and he obviously wasn't able to play, so he figured there needed to be something that could give us that extra 'it' factor, and what could that be?" Woolridge recalled.

Byars was the runner-up to Boston College quarterback Doug Flutie in the Heisman race the previous year, and Byars was the favorite to win it in his senior year. But Byars' foot injury left him off the playing field and Auburn running back Bo Jackson ultimately won the Heisman that year.

"But this particular night, Keith gave an empowering speech that awakened an entire ballroom," Wooldridge said. "Part of his speech, and I guess out of angst, anxiety, the emotion, the excitement and the disappointment of not playing, he swiped at a dinner table and hit glasses and plates and everything and they started breaking everywhere. It was pretty surreal, and at that moment you just felt that *something's happening here*. Something really special is happening right now. And Saturday afternoon, something's going to happen.'"

That something did happen for Wooldridge and the Buckeyes. They found that "it" factor that Byars was hoping to instill in the team during his emotional speech.

made several nice catches. But the Buckeyes still needed to establish a running game.

"We were moving the ball with some good passes, but we weren't really doing what we were capable of doing," Wooldridge said. "In terms of running the ball, we were really getting stymied."

Ohio State didn't look great but they were steady. They opened the scoring with a 28-yard field goal by Rich Spangler and got a safety on a blocked punt by rover back Sonny Gordon with two seconds left in the first quarter that sailed into the back of the end zone for a 5–0 lead.

"The good thing is, our defense kept us in the game," Wooldridge said. "At that moment, I think that sent a reverberation not only through the team, but throughout

> **I** think that sent a reverberation not only through the team, but throughout the stadium.
> —JOHN WOOLDRIDGE

Game Details

Ohio State 22 • Iowa 13

Ohio State	5	10	0	7	**22**
Iowa	0	7	0	6	**13**

Date: November 2, 1985

Team Records: Ohio State 7–1, Iowa 7–1

Scoring Plays:

OSU—Spangler 28-yard FG

OSU—Gordon blocked punt for safety

OSU—Wooldridge 57-yard run (Spangler PAT)

OSU—Spangler 26–yard FG

UI—Harmon 3-yard run (Houghtlin PAT)

OSU—Workman 4-yard run (Spangler PAT)

UI—Hudson 2-yard run (run failed)

the stadium. That blocked punt became infectious to the offense and we finally began to churn out big chunks of yards."

All of a sudden, Coach Bruce turned to Wooldridge, who hadn't played and was barely warmed up on the sideline, and said, "Hey look, we're struggling. Our defense has kept us in it. We've got momentum! We've got to capitalize! Johnny, I need you! *Can you go?*"

Wooldridge, flashing back to a speech Byars gave a day earlier, never hesitated.

"Coach, let's go! I can go!"

Wooldridge entered the game, never feeling any pain from his cracked rib. He hadn't taken any medication; it was all adrenaline. Wooldridge's first offensive play was an isolation running play. Ohio State's fullback George Cooper isolated on the linebacker.

"There was a nose tackle who avoided his block so he was standing right there in the hole when I got the ball," Wooldridge said. "It was almost as if we purposely left him unblocked and he was just standing there. I think he was even surprised. I did a sidestep move, got away from him, and shot right through the line. With the fake, the linebacker and the rest of the defense went with the flow of the fake, I got to the middle of the field and it was wide open. It parted like the Red Sea and I saw nothing but green. I used every bit of my 4.4 speed and it was lights out."

Wooldridge's touchdown made the score 12–0 Ohio State and the Buckeyes never looked back. And as the final seconds ticked off the clock, fans at Ohio Stadium stormed the rain-slicked AstroTurf field to celebrate with the players.

John Wooldridge (25) was a leader on the Buckeye team that won the Fiesta Bowl against Pittsburgh in 1984. *Photo courtesy of AP Images*

October 13, 1984

"Shoeless" Keith

Incredible Run by Keith Byars Even More Impressive Wearing Just One Shoe

Things didn't look good for Ohio State against visiting Illinois. The Buckeyes just couldn't get anything going against the Illini, falling behind 17–0 at the end of the first quarter and 24–0 in the early minutes of the second quarter.

In fact, the 89,937 fans at Ohio Stadium, the second-largest crowd in history at the time, were shocked and disappointed.

"That was an interesting game," said Ohio State running back Johnny Wooldridge. "That was a game that had a lot of changes in momentum. To start that game, everyone in the stadium probably thought Illinois was about to blow us out of Ohio Stadium."

But running back Keith Byars was too much of a competitor to let the Buckeyes get manhandled by Illinois. His amazing afternoon began with a 16-yard touchdown run with 4:13 left in the second quarter, cutting the Illini lead to 24–7.

"I recall Keith coming to the sideline, looking into the CBS camera, and saying, 'We're coming back! We're coming back,'" said Wooldridge, who

had a 75-yard touchdown in the second half called back because of a penalty. "I don't know how many people believed him at the time, but ultimately we began to mount these long drives."

The touchdown capped a 10-play, 91-yard scoring drive and it was the first of *five* touchdowns for Byars as he carried the ball 39 times for 274 yards, breaking Archie Griffin's record of 246 yards against Iowa in 1973. His five touchdowns in the game were also good for a record, tying fullback Pete Johnson.

Wide receiver Cris Carter caught a 30-yard touchdown pass from Mike Tomczak with 3:23 left in the second quarter to cut Illinois' lead to 24–14 and exactly three minutes later, Byars scored his second touchdown, a 4-yard run with 23 seconds left in the half.

At that point, Byars and the Buckeyes could sense the momentum shifting in their favor. Byars struck again early in the third quarter, giving the Buckeyes their first lead of the game at 28–24. His third touchdown of the game, it was a 1-yard run.

Keith Byars surges forward against the Illini in the Buckeyes' 45–38 win.
Photo courtesy of Ohio State University Photo Archives

Illinois cut Ohio State's lead to one point on a field goal midway through the third quarter.

Then came the improbable. Byars scored on a 67-yard touchdown run. Midway through his carry, he lost his left shoe. As he was racing downfield toward the end zone, the crowd went wild. There he was, racing past the Illinois defenders, his loose sock flapping in the wind with every stride he took.

"We were headed into the closed end of the stadium and Keith took the pitch and he went to the right side," Wooldridge said. "He got to the sideline and cut back. What's funny is Keith always wore those low-top Nike turf shoes and almost everyone else, running backs included, wore high-tops because we wanted extra protection on our ankles.

"He was tiptoeing on the sideline and he began to plant his foot and cut back into the middle of the field," Wooldridge said. "When he planted, his shoe slid then flipped off. We used to wear these big, long socks, and oftentimes we would have to fold them under our feet then stick our foot in our shoe. So when his shoe flipped off, he had that sock just flapping and shoe on, or shoe off, no one was going to stop him."

And the Illini didn't.

They couldn't.

After Byars' shoeless touchdown run, the struggle continued. Illinois fought back to tie the score at 35, and then again 38–38. But on the final drive of the game, Byars, Wooldridge, and Tomczak marched Ohio State down the field. The call went again to Byars, who scored the final touchdown of the game, a 3-yard run with 36 seconds left, to clinch the victory.

Game Details

Ohio State 45 • Illinois 38

Illinois	17	7	11	3	**38**
Ohio State	0	21	14	10	**45**

Date: October 13, 1984

Team Records: Illinois 4–3, Ohio State 5–1

Scoring Plays:

UI—Grant 3-yard pass from Trudeau (White PAT)

UI—White 26-yard FG

UI—Williams 9-yard pass from Trudeau (White PAT)

UI— Boso 8-yard pass from Trudeau (White PAT)

OSU—Byars 16-yard run (Spangler PAT)

OSU—Carter 30-yard pass from Tomczak (Spangler PAT)

OSU—Byars 4-yard run (Spangler PAT)

OSU—Byars 1-yard run (Spangler PAT)

UI—White 46-yard FG

OSU—Byars 67-yard run (Spangler PAT)

UI— Wilson 9-yard pass from Trudeau (Trudeau run)

OSU—Spangler 47-yard FG

UI—White 16-yard FG

OSU—Byars 3-yard run (Spangler PAT)

The win put Ohio State in a tie for first place in the Big Ten with Iowa, Michigan, and Purdue. The Buckeyes went on to defeat Michigan 21–6 and earn a trip to the Rose Bowl.

I recall Keith coming to the sideline, looking into the CBS camera, and saying, '"We're coming back! We're coming back!"

—JOHN WOOLDRIDGE

Keith Byars

In 1984 Buckeyes running back Keith Byars gained 2,441 all-purpose yards, including a then-school record 1,764 rushing yards and 22 touchdowns. He was a unanimous first-team All-America selection and voted the Big Ten Conference Most Valuable Player. He was one of the top players in the game and seemed to have a lock on the Heisman. But a Hail Mary pass from a Boston College quarterback named Doug Flutie that iced the Miami Hurricanes propelled Flutie to win the Heisman Trophy in 1984.

Byars was the favorite to win the Heisman in 1985, but a foot injury sidelined him for five games that season. Eager to get back into play, he reinjured his foot in his second game back and missed the remainder of the season. Byars returned for the Citrus Bowl on December 28 against BYU, but hurt his foot in the second offensive series of the game.

Byars never recovered from his chronic foot injury. Many people who knew him have said that the injury prevented him from being the dominant running back he could've been both in his senior year and during his professional career. Still, despite the time lost to injury, Byars finished with 4,369 total yards, 3,200 rushing yards, and 50 touchdowns at Ohio State.

In the NFL, Byars was a punishing runner for the Eagles, Dolphins, Patriots, and Jets.

November 11, 1995

By George, He's Great

Eddie George Races 64 Yards for Score En Route to the Heisman Trophy

It didn't take legendary Ohio State running back Eddie George long to find out what adversity was like at the college level. During his freshman season in a game against Illinois, George experienced trouble holding onto the ball. And that was an understatement. George fumbled the ball at the Illini 4. Not only did Ohio State fail to score a touchdown in a potential scoring situation, but worse, Illinois actually returned the ball 96 yards for a touchdown.

That wasn't the only fumble George had that game. With the Buckeyes trailing by a touchdown, George fumbled the ball at the Illinois 1-yard line. The Illini eventually drove down the field to score the game-winning touchdown.

George's performance against Illinois was the polar opposite of the one he gave two weeks earlier, in a 35–12 win at Syracuse in the Carrier Dome. That Illinois game set the tone for the rest of the season for George because up to that point, he had five touchdowns on 25 carries. He only carried the ball 12 times the rest of the season and did not score a touchdown. It was a grim end to the season.

Flash forward to his senior year against Illinois. Maybe he had something to prove, maybe he wanted to erase the memory of that dismal game three years ago. But boy, did George make it a game to remember at Ohio Stadium.

The Buckeyes were well in control, leading 17–3 midway through the third quarter. They had the ball at their own 36 when George took the handoff from Bobby Hoying and dashed to the left side. Defensive lineman Paul Marshall, who had beaten his blocker and was in the backfield seconds after George took the handoff, had a read on the runner, but George's speed and pure strength helped him elude Marshall. George then got excellent blocks from everyone on the left side of the line—including Orlando Pace and Jamie Sumner, who had simultaneous pancake blocks on their defenders—and the footrace was on, a race that George easily won.

"Ed-die George…Putting up more Heisman numbers!" ABC announcer Brent Musberger exclaimed on national television.

"I think the play was simply called '27,'" Sumner said. "It was just an outside zone play. I was playing next to the world's greatest left tackle in Orlando Pace so he made my job easy. He and I made some space.

When [George] got into the open field, he was gone.

—JAMIE SUMNER

One of Ohio State's most beloved players, running back Eddie George was awarded the Heisman Trophy in 1995. *Photo courtesy of AP Images*

"The thing I loved about that play was that people would say that Eddie didn't have speed because he was a long strider," Sumner said. "But when he got into the open field, he was gone. I remember the stadium just rocking [throughout] the whole game, and that play put the nail in the coffin. It was just an unbelievable play, and an unbelievable run, and I was glad to be a part of it."

That spectacular touchdown was the first of three scores in the game for George. He also scored twice more in the third quarter, on a 13-yard run and a 13-yard pass to give Ohio State a 38–3 lead.

Kicker Josh Jackson tacked on a 26-yard field goal midway through the fourth quarter as the Buckeyes devoured Illinois 41–3.

Three years after suffering one of his worst collegiate games against the Illini, George got his revenge. He had one of his best collegiate games, rushing for a school record 314 yards.

Game Details

Ohio State 41 • Illinois 3

Illinois	0	0	3	0	**3**
Ohio State	14	3	21	3	**41**

Date: November 11, 1995

Team Records: Ohio State 10–1, Illinois 4–5

Scoring Plays:

OSU—Pearson 4-yard run (Jo. Jackson PAT)

OSU—Stanley 14-yard pass from Hoying (Jo. Jackson PAT)

OSU—Jo. Jackson 20-yard FG

UI—Scheuplein 42-yard FG

OSU—George 64-yard run (Jo. Jackson PAT)

OSU—George 13-yard run (Jo. Jackson PAT)

OSU—George 13-yard pass from Hoying (Jo. Jackson PAT)

OSU—Jo. Jackson 26-yard FG

Eddie George was a four-time Pro Bowler and one-time All-Pro running back in the NFL. *Photo courtesy of AP Images*

King George

The Illinois game in 1995 solidified Eddie George's position as the Heisman Trophy favorite, an award he would eventually receive after his senior season. George had his No. 27 jersey retired by Ohio State on November 10, 2001, at a home game against Purdue.

"I am elated about having my number retired," George said at the time. "To be in the same class as Archie Griffin and the other Heisman winners like Les Horvath (1944), Vic Janowicz (1950), and Howard Cassady (1955) is a tremendous honor. I have received many honors both in college and professionally and this ranks very high on the list."

George's game against Illinois was legendary.

"The game...against Illinois to close my career was ironic because of the trouble I had as a freshman," George said. "I wasn't concerned with breaking any records. I was trying to help my team win. It was all because I stuck with it and knew I could improve. I made many believers in my ability that year, and they rewarded me with the Heisman."

Former Ohio State coach John Cooper added: "He had an awesome performance against Illinois as a senior. He ran for 314 yards, and that was not a weak defense. They had a solid defense and two of their linebackers, Kevin Hardy and Simeon Rice, were drafted in the first round. He proved his dedication to his goals, and the Heisman is proof of that."

George rushed for 1,927 yards that year, a single-season school record, and scored 24 touchdowns, second-most in school history in a season.

George's No. 27 is retired by Ohio State.
Photo courtesy of AP Images

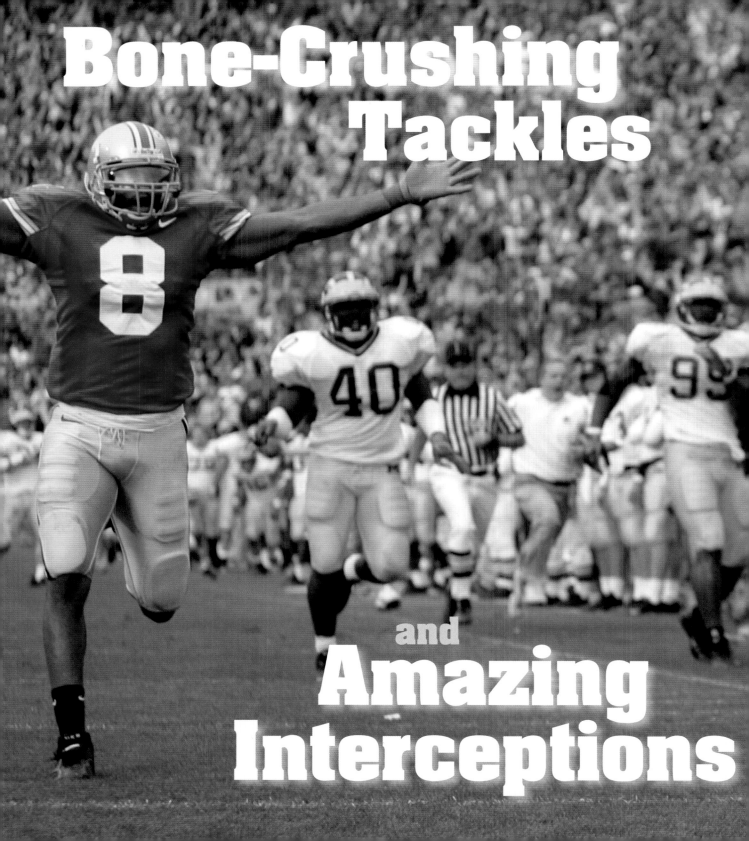

Bone-Crushing Tackles

and Amazing Interceptions

January 3, 2003

The Strip

Maurice Clarett Turns an Ohio State Turnover Into a Miami Turnover in One Play

He wasn't healthy all season. A nagging shoulder injury kept him out of three games during his freshman year. But running back Maurice Clarett still had a sensational season, setting a school record for yards in a season by a freshman with 1,237. He also had 18 touchdowns and averaged an amazing 5.6 yards per carry. His five-yard touchdown run in the 2002 national championship game in double-overtime against favored Miami gave the Buckeyes a 31–24 win.

In that game, Clarett didn't rack up the yards. He finished with just 47 yards on 23 carries but he did score two touchdowns. Instead, it was his *defensive* skills that made one of the biggest plays of the game for the Buckeyes.

Ohio State was inside Miami's 10 and leading 14–7 midway through the third quarter after a 7-yard touchdown run by Clarett with 1:10 left before halftime. Looking to add to the lead in the second half, quarterback Craig Krenzel dropped back to throw and tried to hit a receiver in the end zone who was double-covered. It was one of the very few mistakes Krenzel made the entire game. His ball was intercepted by Miami's Sean Taylor, who ran the ball out of the end zone and shot down the left sideline.

The Buckeyes, with a golden opportunity to take a big lead, let it slip away. Or so it appeared. Clarett wasn't anywhere near the play, but he didn't give up on it. Once he saw the ball was intercepted, he fought off a blocker and chased down Taylor. He caught up with Taylor on the sideline near Miami's 30. In the process of taking Taylor down, Clarett stripped the ball out of Taylor's hands. Ohio State came up with it, giving them possession once again.

"Coach [Tim Spencer] is always talking about, once someone else has the ball, you've got to turn into a defender," Clarett said.

The play was so incredible that legendary ABC college football announcer Keith Jackson didn't realize it was Ohio State's ball until several moments after the play ended. And a television shot showed Krenzel still on the ground after the interception thinking it was Miami's ball.

"That was an outstanding play," Krenzel said. "I was trying to make the tackle and I got blocked so I didn't see what happened. [Clarett] showed what kind of player he was. That gave us a crucial three points."

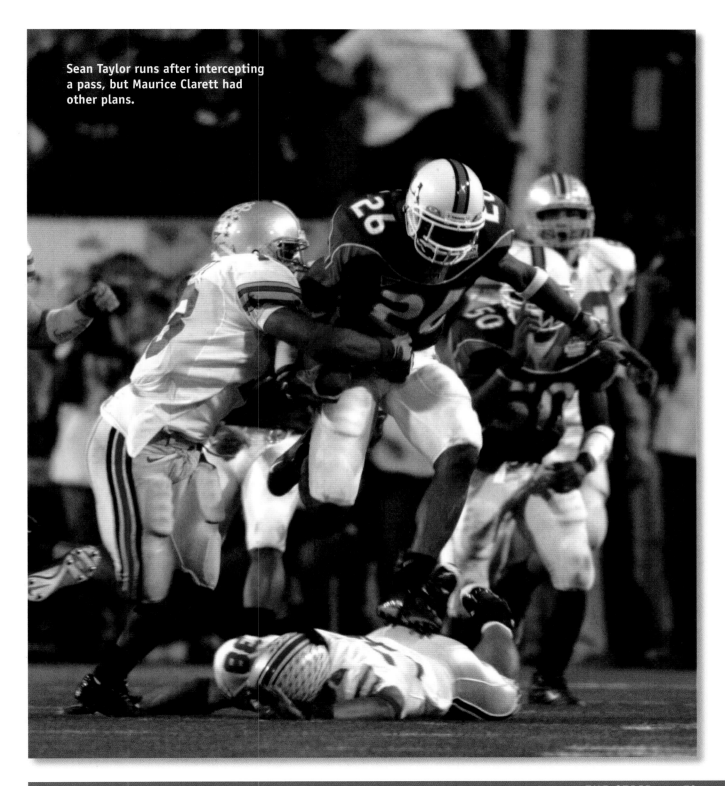

Sean Taylor runs after intercepting a pass, but Maurice Clarett had other plans.

Indeed, the Buckeyes capitalized on Clarett's play. Just four plays later, Mike Nugent kicked a 44-yard field goal with 8:33 left in the third quarter to give Ohio State a 10-point lead.

"That was a huge play. A huge, huge play," Archie Griffin said. "That's the type of player he is. He's been doing that all year."

Coach Tressel agreed.

"Maurice Clarett is a tremendous competitor and gives tremendous effort, as evidenced by the great strip on the interception," Tressel said after the game. "I think he's probably relieved…to be walking out the doors as the national champions."

> **O**nce someone else has the ball, you've got to turn into a defender.
>
> —MAURICE CLARETT

Game Details

Ohio State 31 • Miami 24 (2 OT)

Ohio State	0	14	3	0	14	**31**
Notre Dame	7	0	7	3	7	**24**

Date: January 3, 2003

Team Records: Ohio State 14–0, Miami 12–1

Scoring Plays:

UM—Parrish 25-yard pass from Dorsey (Sievers PAT)

OSU—Krenzel 1-yard run (Nugent PAT)

OSU—Clarett 7-yard run (Nugent PAT)

OSU—Nugent 44-yard FG

UM—McGahee 9-yard run (Sievers PAT)

UM—Sievers 40-yard FG

UM—Winslow 7-yard pass from Dorsey (Sievers PAT)

OSU—Krenzel 1-yard run (Nugent PAT)

OSU—Clarett 5-yard run (Nugent PAT)

The Mind of Maurice Clarett

Winning the national championsip in 2002 was the last great sports moment in Maurice Clarett's life. Soon after the Buckeyes won the title, Clarett's off-the-field troubles began. Myriad legal issues forced him off the Ohio State team, out of college, and into prison, after accepting a plea deal on charges of robbery, carrying a concealed weapon without a permit, and resisting arrest.

While serving time in prison, Clarett started a blog called *The Mind of Maurice Clarett*. Through his blog, he was able to send letters to family members while in prison.

One of Clarett's blog entries showed his newfound and inspiring perspective on eduation and how it holds the key to success for today's youth:

Education, education, education. I am now an advocate of personal education. In order to help the underprivileged and uneducated, I hope that I can position myself to raise the funds and provide those resources to the people from my hometown, Youngstown, Ohio. I believe that in order to change anything you have to invest in people and not places. I know that there are some people back home that see no purpose in educating themselves because they cannot physically see the plus side of education. I hope through the plan I'm putting together I can show them the benefits of getting an education. I understand that I can't help anyone else until I help myself first, that is part of my mission. I want my life to be my testimony and their inspiration. If I can position myself how I envision, I believe my story will be a powerful one. I want to show them that they can move their world with their mind alone. I want to show them the power of words and communication. I also want to show them how to become more aware and conscious of their choices. I believe that since I was exposed to more experiences than others back home that it is my duty to come back and give some advice with education and/or sports. There is more to life than what was taught to me growing up in my neighborhood. The kids in my neighborhood need hope and it all starts with an education.

Maurice Clarett (13) celebrates after wresting the ball back from Sean Taylor.

November 22, 1975

Griffin Is Ohio State Hero

Defensive Back Ray Griffin—Not Brother and Running Back Archie Griffin—Is Man of the Hour

From an offensive statistical standpoint, Michigan outproduced Ohio State. The Wolverines, playing at home, outgained Ohio State 361 to 208 in total yards and ran 77 total plays to the Buckeyes' 61. But none of that mattered to Ohio State. This game came down to one big play at the crucial time. And it was former tailback–turned–defensive back Ray Griffin, the brother and teammate of two-time Heisman Trophy winner Archie Griffin, who came up with the legendary play.

With the score tied at 14 after a 1-yard touchdown run by Buckeyes fullback Pete Johnson with 3:18 remaining, the Big Ten title was on the line. Michigan needed to score, instead of settling for a tie, noted Ohio State football historian Jack Park explained.

"Now the pressure is on Michigan," Park said in a television interview, describing the

scenario years later. "Nobody wants a tie. But because Ohio State has a better nonconference record than Michigan, should the game end in a tie, the tiebreaker would be the overall record. And of course, that would put Ohio State in the Rose Bowl, meaning that Michigan would have to go to the Orange Bowl."

Michigan, led by freshman quarterback Rick Leach, needed to throw the ball. Following Johnson's tying touchdown, Michigan came out throwing. Leach was sacked on first down and threw an incomplete pass on second down. Facing a third-and-18 situation, Leach dropped back to pass, looking to throw downfield, but the pass to wide receiver Jim Smith sailed over Smith's head and into the arms of defensive back Griffin.

As a former running back, Griffin's speed and elusiveness enabled him to take the ball from the middle of the field, all the way down the right sideline. Griffin picked up several key blocks during the return, ultimately getting

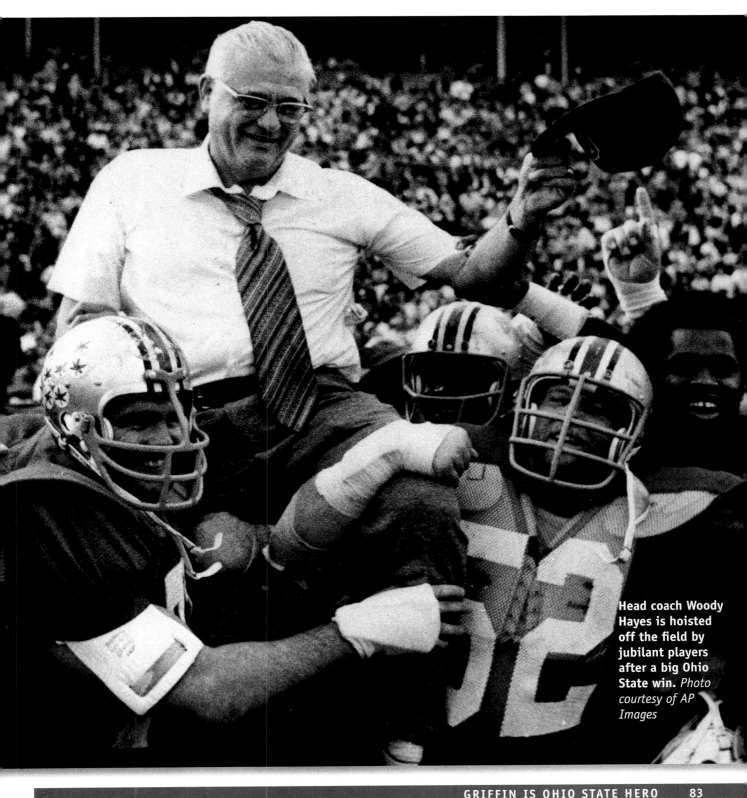

Head coach Woody Hayes is hoisted off the field by jubilant players after a big Ohio State win. *Photo courtesy of AP Images*

The Other Griffin

Raymond James Griffin may have been known as Buckeyes running back Archie Griffin's "little brother," but on November 22, 1975—on the stage of the biggest rivalry in college football, Ohio State vs. Michigan—Ray Griffin made a name for himself.

Ohio State had a reputation that season for its high-powered offense, featuring Archie Griffin, full back Pete Johnson, and Big Ten MVP quarterback Cornelius Green. The older Griffin had gone 31 straight games with at least 100 yards.

Not on this day, though. The Wolverines shut Archie down. Sensing that the outcome of the game was likely going to be determined by which team had the ball last, the Buckeyes defense knew they had to step up big. Ray Griffin did with his key interception, the only one he notched that season. He also finished with 14 total tackles that day, 10 of them solos. Buckeyes defensive backfield coach Dick Walker called Griffin's performance "one of the truly great games a defensive back ever played for Ohio State."

An All-American cornerback, Griffin was taken in the second round of the 1978 draft by the Cincinnati Bengals, where he played seven seasons for them, from 1978 to 1984.

In 2000, Griffin was named to the Ohio State Football All-Century Team that was chosen by the Touchdown Club of Columbus. The All-Century Team is composed of an 80-man roster and a five-man coaching staff. Living members of the team elected Archie Griffin and quarterback Rex Kern as captains on offense and linebacker Chris Spielman and safety Jack Tatum as captains on defense.

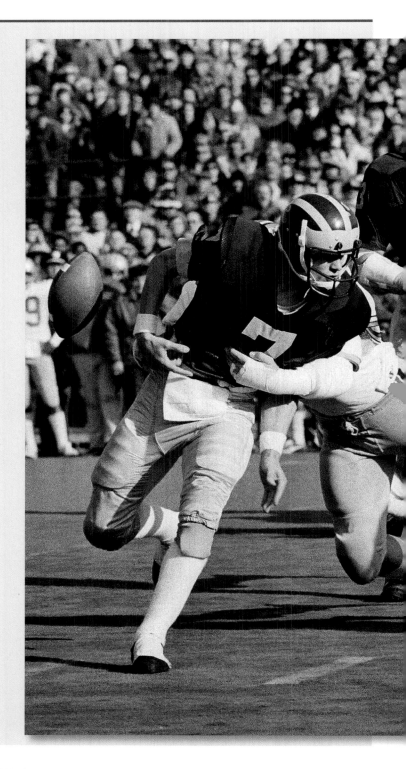

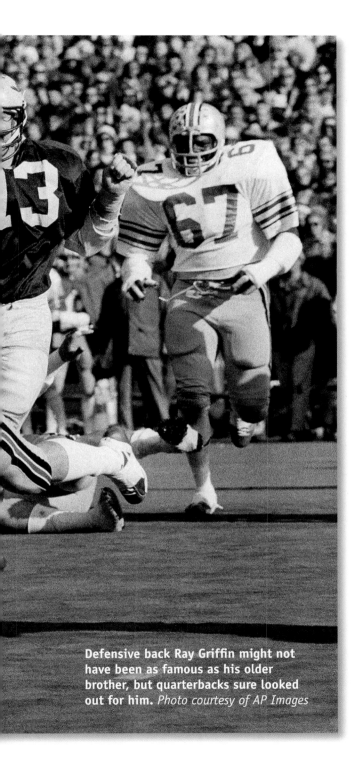

Defensive back Ray Griffin might not have been as famous as his older brother, but quarterbacks sure looked out for him. *Photo courtesy of AP Images*

forced out of bounds by Leach at Michigan's 3-yard line. Indeed, had it not been for Leach, Griffin would have scored.

It only took one play for Johnson, then the nation's leading scorer, to punch it in, giving Ohio State the game-winning touchdown with 2:19 left. It would be all the Buckeyes needed.

The turn of events stunned the Michigan crowd.

"Here you have an Ohio State team that had gone two and a half quarters without a single first down," Park said. "And all of a sudden, within a span of 59 seconds, they had scored two touchdowns."

Michigan still had a chance to drive downfield to tie the game in the final two minutes, but Leach threw another interception. This time it was picked off by Craig Cassady, the son of OSU Heisman Trophy winner "Hopalong" Cassady, and that sealed the victory and an undefeated regular season for the No. 1–ranked Buckeyes.

> **N**obody wants a tie.
>
> —JACK PARK

Game Details

Ohio State 21 • Michigan 14

Michigan	0	7	0	7	**14**
Ohio State	7	0	0	14	**21**

Date: November 22, 1975

Team Records: Ohio State 11–0, Michigan 8–1–2

Scoring Plays:

OSU—Johnson 7-yard pass from Greene (Klaban PAT)

UM—Smith 11-yard pass from Bell (Wood PAT)

UM—Leach 1-yard run (Wood PAT)

OSU—Johnson 1-yard run (Klaban PAT)

OSU—Johnson 3-yard run (Klaban PAT)

September 13, 2003

Packing a Lunch and Working Overtime

The Buckeyes Stand Strong in Three Overtimes to Win

One thing about Jim Tressel's coaching philosophy, even dating back to his 15 years as head coach at Youngstown State University, was that his teams were always defensively tough, from a physical and mental standpoint. Buckeyes fans saw that firsthand with Ohio State's fourth-and-goal stop against the Miami Hurricanes in the 2002 Tostitos Fiesta Bowl to win the national championship. And they saw it the following year in an early-season matchup against North Carolina State in Columbus—a contest that the Buckeyes won 44–38 in triple overtime.

The game lasted nearly 4½ hours, an outcome that didn't seem likely when the Buckeyes, who entered the game ranked No. 3 in the country, led No. 24–ranked North Carolina State 24–7 with 11:25 left to play, following a 6-yard touchdown run by Buckeyes quarterback Craig Krenzel.

But the Wolfpack had quarterback Philip Rivers, who would go on to be a first-round draft pick in the 2004 draft (he was taken by the New York Giants then traded to the San Diego Chargers in exchange for Eli Manning). It was Rivers' play (he was 36-of-52 for 315 yards, four touchdowns and two interceptions), especially in the fourth quarter, that helped spark a North Carolina State comeback.

Rivers hit T.J. Williams on a 5-yard touchdown pass with 21 seconds remaining to tie the score at 24. The touchdown capped an eight-play, 86-yard scoring drive that was precisely orchestrated and executed by Rivers. The score also sent the game into overtime, the first overtime game in the 81-year history of Ohio Stadium.

"I still say to this day, I'm not sure I've played against a better quarterback than Philip Rivers," Tressel told the Big Ten Network in 2008. "I thought, going into the game, he was special. And I thought afterward he was even more special."

Officials confer over NC State tailback T.A. McClendon and confirm the onfield ruling that he was stopped short of the goal line by Buckeyes defenders. *Photo courtesy of AP Images*

But what was truly special about the game was the Buckeyes' defense and their ability to come up with the big stop to win the game. On fourth-and-goal at the 1-yard line, North Carolina State trailed by six points. They had a chance to score to tie the game; they could even win with a two-point conversion.

NC State ran quarterback sneaks on first down and again on third down, but the Buckeyes played it perfectly, holding their ground. On fourth down, the Wolfpack lined up four receivers to the right, leaving T.A. McLendon as the lone running back. McLendon, a big, bruising back, took the pitch and went left. He made his cut and charged toward the goal line. With his speed and power, it appeared that he would ramble into the end zone.

Buckeyes linebacker A.J. Hawk got to the line of scrimmage and tried to get an arm on McLendon, but

he couldn't stop the powerful running back. Defensive back Will Allen came up huge with the tackle that saved the game. Allen lowered his shoulder into McLendon just before McLendon made it to the goal line. The running back fell backwards onto the turf as he tried to stretch the ball across the goal. After several moments of discussion by the officials, they ruled that McLendon hit the ground before he crossed the goal line. The game was over.

The Buckeyes escaped with an historic win and extended their winning streak to 17 games, which stretched back to their national championship season in 2002.

"We knew that we still had that...that we could still go into a game, play a good team, play a close game," quarterback Craig Krenzel told the Big Ten Network. "Whatever it took...we still had that ability to lean on each other that

Head coach Jim Tressel sings "Carmen, Ohio" with players after the Buckeyes' triple-overtime defeat of NC State.
Photo courtesy of AP Images

somehow, some way, we are going to get the job done and that was kind of our motto and the way we played."

Defensive end Tim Anderson said, "It's obviously a great confidence boost. Philip Rivers' teams are expected to do well. There could've been a lot of excuses we could've made for losing that game…and I think that was good and the fact that we did finish out the game and finished out strong."

The Buckeyes finished the season 11–2 and dominated Kansas State 35–28 in the 2004 Fiesta Bowl. But the North Carolina State win was special in many ways for Tressel.

"…Vivid recall of fourth down, we're up by six. If they score they have a chance to get the six and go for two and

beat us," Tressel said. "You saw the likes of A.J. Hawk and Will Allen and those guys flying there to make the hit and bend [McLendon] six inches shy. We still have a large photo of that hanging on the walls of our football facility because it was one of those gut-check plays."

Never Surrender

Ohio State defensive lineman Will Smith was a man who always strived for perfection during his outstanding career at Ohio State. So when the Buckeyes let a 17-point fourth-quarter lead slip away at home, you could understand his frustration.

"Everybody got complacent in this game when it was 24–7 in the fourth quarter," Smith told the *Cincinnati Enquirer* after the game. "Everybody said, 'Oh, this game's over.'" And Smith was right. It wasn't over. But Ohio State's defense held strong and got the job done with its stop of running back T.A. McLendon, on fourth-and-goal at the 1.

"I saw an opening," McLendon said after the game, describing the moment when he took the pitch from quarterback Philip Rivers, went to his left, then tried to punch it past the goal line. "I don't know who hit me, but I fell with my arms in the air. I think I have it every play, but I guess I didn't here."

But before Ohio State's defensive stop, Buckeyes quarterback Craig Krenzel issued a challenge to his team in the huddle, when the Buckeyes got the ball for the game-winning drive in the third overtime.

"That's one of the reasons we come here. It's the tradition and the type of games you're going to play in," Krenzel told the *Enquirer*. "I brought that up and said, 'Let's go do our jobs.'"

Tressel told the *Enquirer*: "Our guys never stop playing. They never stop believing they have a chance. College overtime is extraordinary. It's great football."

Game Details

Ohio State 44 • North Carolina 38 (3 OT)

North Carolina	0	7	0	17	14	**38**
Ohio State	14	0	3	7	20	**44**

Date: September 13, 2003

Team Records: Ohio State 3–0, North Carolina 1–2

Scoring Plays:

OSU—Jenkins 44-yard pass from Krenzel (Nugent PAT)

OSU—Ross 2-yard run (Nugent PAT)

NCST—Cotchery 11-yard pass from Rivers (Kiker PAT)

OSU—Nugent 22-yard FG

OSU—Krenzel 6-yard run (Nugent PAT)

NCST—Cotchery 9-yard pass from Rivers (Kiker PAT)

NCST—Kiker 24-yard FG

NCST—Williams 5-yard pass from Rivers (Kiker PAT)

OSU—Hartsock 10-yard pass from Krenzel (Nugent PAT)

NCST—Hall 17-yard pass from Rivers (Kiker PAT)

NCST—McLendon 2-yard run (Kiker PAT)

OSU—Hamby 2-yard pass from Krenzel (Nugent PAT)

OSU—Jenkins 7-yard pass from Krenzel (pass failed)

October 26, 2002

What a Gamble

Chris Gamble Makes Yet Another Game-Changing Play to Keep the Buckeyes Undefeated

On October 19, 2002, Ohio State kicker Mike Nugent booted two field goals at Wisconsin, propelling the Buckeyes over the Badgers 19–14. All-purpose player sophomore Chris Gamble—a cornerback, wide receiver, and kick returner for the Buckeyes—also had a hand in the win, intercepting the Badgers in the end zone on Wisconsin's final drive.

Flash forward one week. No. 4–ranked Ohio State was hosting Penn State. The Buckeyes looked to extend their winning streak to nine games. And once again, close games seemed to be Ohio State's calling card. But also once again, and luckily for the Buckeyes, Gamble—the Buckeye's first two-way starter in 39 years—was able to come up with the game-clinching play.

Penn State led 7–3 facing a third-and-12 at its own 17 with just over 13 minutes left in the third quarter. Ohio State had a three-man front with Will Smith standing at the line of scrimmage and showing blitz.

Penn State quarterback Zack Mills dropped back in the shotgun, took the snap, and rolled to his left looking for a receiver. He threw a weak pass on the run that looked like it was *just waiting* to be intercepted. And it was.

Gamble appeared from out of nowhere and jumped in front of the intended receiver near the right sideline, snatching the ball. But what he did *after* the interception was even more remarkable. Taking that floating pass at the Nittany Lions' 40, he set off on a foot race to the end zone. He made several cuts to elude tacklers, running the ball like a veteran running back, and knifed his way into the end zone on a spectacular return that gave Ohio State the lead with 13:07 left in the third quarter.

"I saw Zack Mills rolling to the left, the one dude running the post, and the other dude running the wheel [pattern]," said Gamble, who became the first Ohio State player since Paul Warfield in 1963 to start both ways. "I saw [Mills] throw it to the wheel, and I just attacked it," Gamble said.

Coach Jim Tressel added, "Chris Gamble's a great player, but he's [also] a smart player. There's a lot of talented players in the world, but they all don't have a feel for the game. He's blessed with talent, and he pays close attention to what's going on on the field."

Chris Gamble was
the difference in the
Buckeyes' 2002 contest
against the Badgers.

Double Trouble

What do Chuck Bednarik, Deion Sanders, and William "the Refrigerator" Perry all have in common? They were all two-way starters in the NFL. "The Fridge," who played defensive line, wasn't your typical two-way starter, but he was routinely used as a goal-line fullback by Chicago Bears coach Mike Ditka and even scored a touchdown in Super Bowl XX.

Chris Gamble arrived at OSU to play wide receiver and ended his career as a prolific two-way starter, playing receiver and defensive back, and even returning kicks. He could hurt a team in almost every phase of the game.

Gamble left Ohio State after his junior year to enter the NFL draft. He ended his career with the Buckeyes with 19 starts at cornerback, 14 starts at wide receiver, and six games starting at both positions, the first player in 39 years to start at OSU on both sides of the line of scrimmage.

Opposing coaches could never be sure how Gamble would impact the game. He could catch the ball and streak by a defender, he could step in front of a pass and return it for a touchdown, or he could field a punt and give his team great field position.

Gamble was drafted by the Carolina Panthers, the 28th pick overall in the 2004 NFL Draft.

Gamble, shown here with the Carolina Panthers, brings new meaning to the term "all-purpose."
Photo courtesy of AP Images

Culminating an impressive 14-play, 72-yard drive that chewed 8:21 off the clock, Nugent kicked a 37-yard field goal with 1:05 left in the third quarter to give the Buckeyes a 13–7 lead.

The Buckeyes' defense, meanwhile, did its own outstanding job. Nittany Lions running back Larry Johnson finished with a measly 66 yards on 16 carries—this after rushing for a school-record 257 yards a week earlier in a big win against Northwestern. Quarterback Mills was just 14-of-28 for 98 yards and threw three interceptions.

There wasn't much legendary Penn State coach Joe Paterno could say after the game, except, "We got licked."

> **I** saw [Mills] throw it to the wheel, and I just attacked it.
>
> —CHRIS GAMBLE

Game Details

Ohio State 13 • Penn State 7

Penn State	7	0	0	0	**7**
Ohio State	0	3	10	0	**13**

Date: October 26, 2002

Team Records: Ohio State 9–0, Penn State 5–3

Scoring Plays:

PSU—Johnson 5-yard run (Gould PAT)

OSU—Nugent 37-yard FG

OSU—Gamble 40-yard interception return (Nugent PAT)

OSU—Nugent 37-yard FG

Michigan head coach Bo Schembechler and Ohio State head coach Woody Hayes enjoyed a longstanding friendship and rivalry. *Photo courtesy of AP Images*

November 17, 1979

A Tale of Two Coaches

A Late Touchdown on Special Teams Gives Hayes' Ohio State Win Against Rival Schembechler's Michigan

Many football minds—including current Buckeyes coach Jim Tressel—maintain that the most important play in football is the punt, because there are so many variables that need to align for it to be a successful play, and so many things that can cause the play to go wrong. The play has the potential to quickly shift the momentum of a game with the shift of field position.

And that's precisely how the game played out in Ohio State's battle against Michigan in Ann Arbor in 1979. Junior defensive back Todd Bell scooped up a blocked punt by Jim Laughlin at the 18 and raced into the end zone for the touchdown, which gave the Buckeyes an 18–15 win. The crowd of 106,255 fans—the largest crowd at the time to ever watch a regular-season game—was stunned.

> **I**f I were the greatest high school kicker in the country, I'd contact Schembechler because he's *definitely* interested.
>
> **—BO SCHEMBECHLER**

In the November 26, 1979 edition of *Sports Illustrated*, there was quarterback Art Schlichter on the cover, an action shot of him in the Michigan win. The title of the cover story read, "Buckeye Block Party."

After the game, Michigan coach Bo Schembechler told *Sports Illustrated*, "The point is that our kicking game has been disastrous. With a decent kicker, well, I don't say we'd be undefeated, but we'd sure be better. I'll tell you, if I were the greatest high school kicker in the country, I'd contact Schembechler because he's *definitely* interested."

Trailing 15–12 at the time, it didn't seem like a "party" for first-year head coach Earle Bruce and the Buckeyes. Bruce knew his team needed to come up with a big play. Bell was the hero for scoring the game-winning touchdown and his Johnny-on-the-spot reaction to the play was outstanding. But Laughlin and the rest of the 10-man Ohio State defensive front earned praise for the design play. Laughlin came in from the left side of the line and blocked Bryan Virgil's punt.

Incidentally, it was Ohio State safety Vince Skillings who had the first shot at picking up the blocked punt—but he kicked it, and the ball took a perfect bounce right into the waiting arms of Bell. The win helped the Buckeyes finish the season undefeated and untied for the first time since 1975.

Ohio State got on the board first with a 23-yard field goal by Vlade Janakievski late in the second quarter. Then the Wolverines took a 7–3 lead with 1:30 left in the quarter on a 59-yard touchdown pass from Johnny Wangler to wide receiver Anthony Carter. But the Buckeyes chipped away at the lead with just 30 second left before halftime on a 25-yard field goal by Janakievski.

Midway through the third quarter, Ohio State quarterback Art Schlichter helped give the Buckeyes a 12–7 lead

Game Details

Ohio State 18 • Michigan 15

Michigan	0	7	8	0	**15**
Ohio State	0	6	6	6	**18**

Date: November 17, 1979

Team Records: Michigan 8–3, Ohio State 11–0

Scoring Plays:

OSU—Janakievski 23-yard FG

UM—Carter 59-yard pass from Wangler (Virgil PAT)

OSU—Janakievski 25-yard FG

OSU—Hunter 18-yard pass from Schlichter (PAT failed)

UM—Smith 1-yard run (Smith run)

OSU—Bell 18-yard blocked punt return (PAT failed)

on an 18-yard touchdown pass to wide receiver Chuck Hunter, but the two-point conversion failed.

The Wolverines took their last lead of the game with 3:38 left in the third quarter when running back Roosevelt Smith scored on a 1-yard run, then added the two-point conversion run.

Both defenses held, as neither team's offenses scored the rest of the game. So it was fitting that Ohio State's entire defensive unit won the game for the Buckeyes and sent them to the Rose Bowl for the first time since '75.

Meanwhile, the loss sent Michigan to the Gator Bowl to face North Carolina, led defensively by future NFL Hall of Fame linebacker Lawrence Taylor. The Wolverines lost to the Tar Heels 17–15, after failing a two-point conversion attempt left with less than two minutes remaining.

At Ohio Stadium, in the 81st meeting between Michigan and Ohio State, Earle Bruce, a coach who never got the breaks or respect he deserved, put together a surprising game plan.

—MIKE LANESE FROM *GAME OF MY LIFE*

Saved by the Bell

It was 1979 and Pete Carroll—yes, that Pete Carroll—was the secondary coach for Earl Bruce's Buckeyes. Long before his defenses were making big plays at USC, Carroll's OSU secondary was making big plays throughout the '79 season—and none may bigger than that blocked punt and subsequent 18-yard touchdown return for a touchdown by defensive back Todd Bell.

Ohio State coach Earle Bruce made the biggest call of the game. All year long the Buckeyes punt rush teams were getting through virtually untouched by the blockers on the punt coverage teams. Jim Laughlin had been the main culprit, rushing from the right side of the defense. So, figuring that Michigan had prepared for that situation, Bruce moved Laughlin to the left side. And Laughlin, Ben Lee, and Mike D'Andrea rushed through untouched.

After the game, Bell was seen with a big smile and wearing a button that read "Praise the Lord." Later that season, in the Rose Bowl, Bell ran down Heisman Trophy winner and USC running back Charles White from behind and stripped the ball from him to prevent a touchdown—another stellar play in the annals of Ohio State football lore.

In 1981 Bell was drafted in the fourth round by the Chicago Bears. He played in Chicago through the 1987 season, and finished out his career in Philadelphia in 1989. Bell was a Pro Bowl selection in 1984.

Tragically, just before 7:00 AM on March 16, 2005, while driving in Reynoldsburg, Ohio, just south of Columbus, Bell suffered an apparent heart attack, lost control of his vehicle, and was later pronounced dead at the age of 46.

Bell (left) was a solid player in the NFL. Here, with Philadelphia, he clobbers Bears running back Neal Anderson in 1988 game action. *Photo courtesy of AP Images*

November 23, 2002

Where There's a Will...

Buckeyes Defensive Back Will Allen Intercepts
Pass on Final Play To Help Beat Michigan

He was "Teflon Tressel," the never-let-'em-see-you-sweat guy, right to the end.

And so it was Coach Jim Tressel's demeanor as he watched the final seven seconds of the game against Michigan tick away. It all came down to the last moments. Ohio State's 29th Big Ten title was on the line. More importantly, an undefeated regular season and a trip to the national championship were at stake, the first for the Buckeyes since 1968.

"I took my headset off with seven seconds left and said, 'Come on, D,'" Tressel told the *Los Angeles Times*.

Those final seconds seemed like an eternity to linebacker Matt Wilhelm. Michigan quarterback John Navarre threw an incomplete pass in the back of the end zone, but the clock stopped with one second left. It was the first year in which the NCAA implemented independent clock operators, so there was no "home clock" to blame for keeping the Wolverines' hopes alive.

Even so, Wilhelm wasn't happy that the Wolverines had one last shot at the end zone and the win. "My only thought was, *Who's the guy running the clock?*" Wilhelm told the *Cleveland Plain Dealer*. "I mean, one second left! What is that?"

Celebration erupts on the Buckeyes sideline as Will Allen comes up huge.

On the next play, Navarre dropped back once again to pass, on fourth-and-10 at Ohio State's 24. He was looking at wide receiver Braylon Edwards, who was lined up on the far left of the line of scrimmage. Edwards ran a simple post pattern and Navarre tried to squeeze the ball through two defenders but Will Allen never let Edwards get behind him. Allen just stepped in front of Edwards, right at the goal line, and picked off the pass—giving the Buckeyes the win, an undefeated regular season, another Big Ten title, and a berth in the BCS Tostitos National Championship game.

"When Will made the interception, I just started crying," said Buckeyes strong safety Mike Doss. Ohio State's defense had stepped up all year. This was just one more stellar performance. The Buckeyes' defense did not give up a touchdown in the game, holding Michigan to just three Adam Finley field goals.

Ohio State's offense was outgained 368 to 264, but Buckeyes freshman running back Maurice Clarett—who had been bothered by a shoulder injury for most of the season (he missed three games that season due to the injury)—still rushed for 119 yards on 20 carries. "I'll tell you, he's a tough kid," Tressel said about Clarett. "We talked early in the week and he was going to play. There was no doubt."

Clarett's two-yard touchdown run in the first quarter gave the Buckeyes a 7–3 lead. Finley kicked two more field goals. His second with 16 seconds left in the second quarter gave the Wolverines a 9–7 halftime lead. The Buckeyes went ahead 14–9 on Maurice Hall's three-yard touchdown run with 4:55 remaining in the game, setting up the dramatic finish.

Moments after the game, ABC sideline reporter Jack Arute managed to catch Tressel in the midst of Ohio State's celebration.

"Coach, you're headed to the national championship, congratulations," Arute said. In typical fashion, Tressel tried downplaying the obvious.

"Well, I don't know if that's for sure, but I'm sure proud that Ohio State won in the big rivalry," Tressel said. "And I'll tell you what, we're so proud of our kids. They played like crazy. That's the Ohio State–Michigan game…It's awful special, we got great kids, we got great coaches, and how about these fans."

> **M**y only thought was, *Who's the guy running the clock?*
>
> —MATT WILHELM

Game Details

Ohio State 14 • Michigan 9

Michigan	3	6	0	0	**9**
Ohio State	7	0	0	7	**14**

Date: November 23, 2002

Team Records: Michigan 9–3, Ohio State 13–0

Scoring Plays:
UM—Finley 36-yard FG
OSU—Clarett 2-yard run (Nugent PAT)
UM—Finley 36-yard FG
UM—Finley 22-yard FG
OSU—Hall 3-yard run (Nugent PAT)

Will Allen

Ohio State defensive back Will Allen delivered many big plays during his career at Ohio State. The four-year letter winner for the Buckeyes was a consensus first-team All-America selection in his senior year, playing behind three-time All-American strong safety Mike Doss. Still, Allen was an effective defensive back who saw action on the field primarily in nickel coverage on passing downs.

In the annals of Ohio State, Allen is probably best known for two very memorable plays. The first was his interception on a pass by Michigan quarterback John Navarre that gave the Buckeyes a 14–9 victory, cemented an undefeated regular season, and sent the team to the national championship game against the Miami Hurricanes in 2002.

The other memorable play happened in the Buckeyes' next game—the BCS Tostitos Fiesta Bowl. In the second half of that game, Allen charged Miami running back Willis McGahee, driving his helmet into the runner's knee on a clean and legal hit. Neutralizing the runner was a key component of the Buckeyes' ultimate BCS victory in that game.

Will Allen epitomized class on and off the field.

October 12, 1968

Pick Six

Ted Provost and "Super Sophomores" Propel Woody Hayes' Buckeyes to Victory Over Boilermakers

Legendary Ohio State coach Woody Hayes saw countless dramatic, inspiring, last-second wins during his illustrious career with the Buckeyes. But watching his team completely dominate the No. 1–ranked Purdue Boilermakers, a 14-point favorite led by quarterback Mike Phipps, was a special moment in Hayes' storied career. The Buckeyes shut out Purdue 13–0 in a stellar defensive display.

"It was the greatest effort I've ever seen," Hayes said.

It was All-American defensive back Ted Provost's 34-yard interception return for a touchdown in the third quarter that broke a scoreless tie and proved to be the game-winner.

During an Ohio State alumni event years later, Provost told author Mark Rea that he never gets tired of Ohio State fans coming up to him and asking him about that play. After scoring the touchdown, Provost threw the ball into the stands in excitement. Rea asked Provost if he was afraid to face Hayes once he reached the sideline.

"No," Provost said. "[Defensive backfield coach Lou Holtz] told us that if we scored, we could do it. I just got caught up in the emotion, I guess."

The win was so special for Ohio State because Purdue, on paper, shouldn't have had any problem handling the fourth-ranked Buckeyes. The Boilermakers averaged more than 40 points a game that season, and had easily defeated Ohio State the year before. Coming into the game, Hayes was still upset about that 41–6 loss in '67.

"They could have beaten us 60–0 that day," Provost told Rea. "We just got humiliated in the secondary. They wiped us out. And it made Woody point to that game for the whole next year. Usually it was Michigan that we thought about all summer. That year it was Purdue. We had those guys' [jersey] numbers taped up on

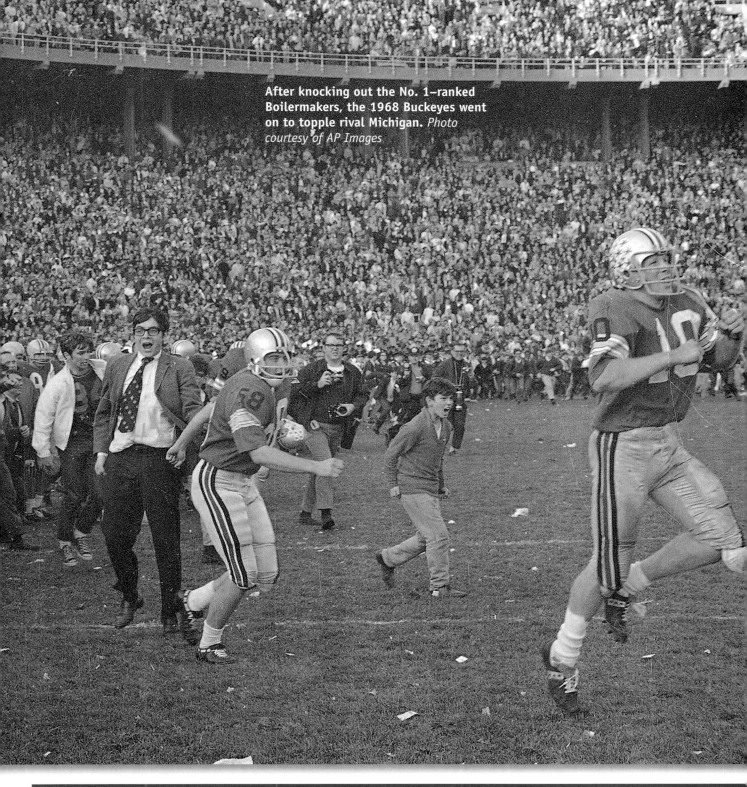

After knocking out the No. 1–ranked Boilermakers, the 1968 Buckeyes went on to topple rival Michigan. *Photo courtesy of AP Images*

Hayes confers with quarterback Rex Kern during game action.

Coming Up Roses

Ohio State started the 1968 season ranked No. 11 in the country, but there was a lot of optimism within the team and among the Buckeye Nation—for good reason. The Buckeyes were returning a host of starters from the '67 season, in which they went 5–2 in the Big Ten and 6–3 overall. They finished 4–0 at home that year and defeated Michigan 24–14 in Ann Arbor. All in all, it was a positive way to end the season and prepare for the coming year.

OSU's star fullback, Jim Otis, was back, along with a group of talented underclassmen including defensive back Ted Provost, quarterback Rex Kern, running back John Brockington, safety Jack Tatum, and defensive linemen Jim Stillwagon, just to name a few of the "Super Sophomores." It wouldn't be long before the Buckeyes started making their move toward the top of the polls.

Defeating then–No. 1 Purdue 13–0 in Columbus was just one of the highlights of the season. Another was drubbing No. 4–ranked Michigan 50–14, after the Wolverines trailed just 20–14 at halftime.

Top-ranked Ohio State then met No. 2 USC in the Rose Bowl. The Buckeyes trailed the Trojans 10–0 on an 80-yard touchdown run by O.J. Simpson. But that short-lived USC lead did not faze the undaunted Buckeyes one bit. They piled on 27 unanswered points and dominated USC in a 27–16 victory to win the Rose Bowl and the national championship. Fittingly, Woody Hayes was named the Coach of the Year by the Associated Press.

our lockers, we had their faces taped on the mirrors in the locker room. We saw those guys in our sleep."

That's why the '68 season for the Buckeyes and the Purdue matchup in Columbus was so important. It was going to be Ohio State's year; the Buckeyes' opponents hadn't gotten the memo.

Phipps and Boilermakers star running back Leroy Keyes struggled against Ohio State's defense all afternoon. Phipps threw for just 106 yards and was sacked four times. Keyes was held to 18 yards, while Buckeyes fullback Jim Otis pounded out 144 yards. Ohio State's other touchdown was a 14-yard touchdown run by backup quarterback Billy Long, filling in for an injured Rex Kern, for the final score later in the third quarter.

The win catapulted Ohio State to No. 2. The Buckeyes didn't reach No. 1 until the 1969 Rose Bowl, when they upset USC 27–16 to win the national championship. But for the undefeated Buckeyes, none of those wins were upsets in their minds.

> **It was the greatest effort I've ever seen.**
> —WOODY HAYES

Game Details

Ohio State 13 • Purdue 0

Purdue	0	0	0	0	**0**
Ohio State	0	0	13	0	**13**

Date: October 12, 1968

Team Records: Ohio State 3–0, Purdue 3–1

Scoring Plays:

OSU—Provost 34-interception return (PAT failed)

OSU—Long 14-yard run (Roman PAT)

I didn't see him going for the flag and I thought, *He ain't going to throw it.*

—CHRIS GAMBLE

Hurricanes players prematurely celebrate victory in the BCS National Championship Game. *Photo courtesy of AP Images*

January 3, 2003

The Call Heard Around the World

Late Penalty Against Miami Keeps Buckeyes' National Championship Hopes Alive

Miami Hurricanes fans will talk about "the Call" forever. And so will Ohio State Buckeyes fans. It was a pass interference call against Miami defensive back Glenn Sharpe in the 2002 BCS National Championship Game on fourth and 3 at the 5-yard line that kept Ohio State's drive alive, gave the Buckeyes the ball on the 1-yard line, and granted Coach Jim Tressel and the Buckeye Nation another chance.

Ohio State was trailing 24–17 in the first overtime and needed a touchdown to force a second overtime period. Trying to win their first national championship since 1968, the Buckeyes were also vying to become the first Division I-A school in history to go undefeated in a season and win 14 games.

Buckeyes quarterback Craig Krenzel was in shotgun formation, and the lone player in the backfield for the Buckeyes. Wide receiver Chris Gamble was flanked wide-right along with Michael Jenkins. Even running back Maurice Clarett was lined up on the line of scrimmage, on the far-left side.

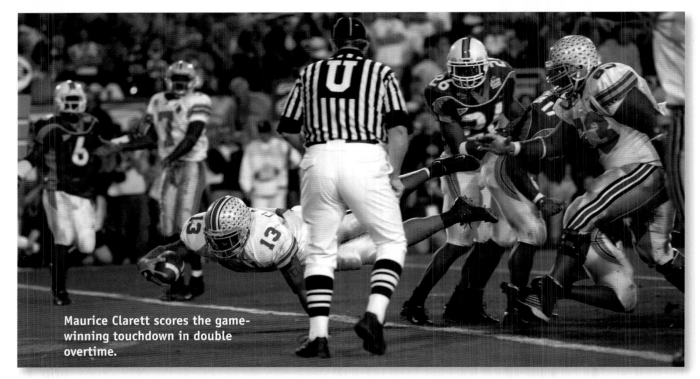

Maurice Clarett scores the game-winning touchdown in double overtime.

Krenzel took the snap and was looking at Gamble the whole time. Gamble, who had several game-winning plays during the course of the regular season that helped put the Buckeyes in the national championship game, was closely guarded by Sharpe. Krenzel was hoping to connect with Gamble for yet another dramatic play. With a defender moments from sacking him, Krenzel threw the pass to Gamble in the right corner of the end zone.

Just as Krenzel released the ball, he took a crushing blow that sent him to the turf on his back. He didn't get a chance to see what had transpired as the pass fell incomplete. The Miami Hurricanes started to rush the field, thinking the game was over. Gamble was pleading to the officials in the end zone that he was interfered with while trying to make the catch.

"He was holding me," Gamble said. "He was in my face mask and my shoulder pads. I was waiting for the flag, but he kind of hesitated. I didn't see him going for the flag and I thought, *He ain't going to throw it.* Luckily, he did, and I'm like, *Whew.*"

Game Details

Ohio State 31 • Miami 24 (2 OT)

Ohio State	0	14	3	0	14	**31**
Miami	7	0	7	3	7	**24**

Date: January 3, 2003

Team Records: Ohio State 14–0, Miami 12–1

Scoring Plays:

UM—Parrish 25-yard pass from Dorsey (Sievers PAT)

OSU—Krenzel 1-yard run (Nugent PAT)

OSU—Clarett 7-yard run (Nugent PAT)

OSU—Nugent 44-yard FG

UM— McGahee 9-yard run (Sievers PAT)

UM—Sievers 40-yard FG

UM—Winslow 7-yard pass from Dorsey (Sievers PAT)

OSU—Krenzel 1-yard run (Nugent PAT)

OSU—Clarett 5-yard run (Nugent PAT)

"They Let That One Call Hold Them Back"

For the record, several national newspapers reported that television replays clearly showed Sharpe with a hand on Gamble moments before the ball got there. And as much as the Miami Hurricanes felt that the pass interference call in the 2003 Tostitos BCS National Championship Game gave Ohio State the title, the truth is the Buckeyes still needed to score just to tie the game in overtime and send the game into a second OT.

Craig Krenzel scored on a 1-yard run, then the Buckeyes got the ball first on the second OT and Maurice Clarett scored on a 5-yard run. Miami still had a chance at tying the score and sending the game into a third overtime.

Technically, the game *wasn't* decided on the pass interference call that went in Ohio State's favor. However, that play did shift the momentum in the Buckeyes' favor and Miami wasn't the same after that play.

A South Florida native and former player for Tressel at Youngstown State, Lorenzo Davis gave an interesting opinion on the call and the eventual outcome.

"Ohio State got another chance to redeem itself after the pass interference and they scored," Davis said. "But that wasn't the game-winning touchdown because Miami got the ball back and still got another chance to redeem *themselves* and they didn't. They let that one call hold them back."

Miami did seem to lose the confidence, even if it was slightly, that they had maintained all year. The underdog Buckeyes could sense victory and Krenzel led the way.

"All I know is, Krenzel did for us what we needed done," Tressel said.

"He" was field judge Terry Porter. The referee standing right at the goal line signaled that the play was incomplete and didn't throw a flag. But Porter, who was in the back corner of the end zone, threw the flag several seconds after the ball hit the ground.

"I saw the guy [Sharpe] holding the guy [Gamble] prior to the ball being in the air. He was still holding him, pulling him down while the ball was in the air," Porter said.

When Krenzel finally rose from the ground, he saw that he had a second chance.

"After I threw it, I got hit," Krenzel said. "As I was getting hit, the ball was in the air and I saw contact going on in the corner. The ball fell incomplete, [Miami] rushed the field, and I sat there."

Krenzel said he remembered having a feeling of dejection, thinking the game was over. "I thought there was contact but I didn't see the flag until after I got up. I think it was the right call."

What did Tressel think?

"I thought there was interference but I did not see a flag for a moment," Tressel said. "I thought, *Isn't that a shame*, because I think the ball was thrown well...Craig came up with the thought on the play for Chris to do the route he did. I thought he was interfered with, but I didn't see a flag.

"You know we don't complain about things if they don't go our way," Tressel said. "It was good to see that guy come up in the back of the end zone and make what I thought was a good call."

Once order was restored and the players not actually playing went back to the sideline, Krenzel scored on a 1-yard run on first-and-goal to tie the score at 24, sending the contest into the second overtime.

From there, Clarett scored on a 5-yard run for a 31–24 Ohio State lead and the Buckeyes' defense held the Hurricanes on fourth down to win the national championship. It was definitely one for the ages.

October 23, 1954

"Hopalong" Hops His Way to Ohio State Victory

Cassady and the Buckeyes Defense No Match For Badgers

The matchup between the host Ohio State Buckeyes and the Wisconsin Badgers was big for a couple reasons. First, Wisconsin headed into the game ranked No. 2 in the country. Second, the Badgers boasted Heisman Trophy candidate and fullback Alan Ameche, so the Buckeyes knew they would have their hands full. But Ohio State's defense was strong and the unit rose to the challenge.

Ohio State trailed Wisconsin 7–3 at halftime and all the Buckeyes could muster on offense was a 32-yard field goal late in the first quarter by Tad Weed.

But the momentum shifted in a big way for Ohio State in the third quarter when Howard "Hopalong" Cassady came up with the play of the game. He intercepted a pass and returned

Howard "Hopalong" Cassady (42) was the conquering
hero in OSU's 1954 win over Wisconsin.

"Hopalong" Cassady

There is no doubt that the high point of the 1954 season for Ohio State was winning the Rose Bowl against USC. The conditions during the game were dreadful: cold, rainy, and muddy. Still, the Buckeyes, led by Woody Hayes' run-it-down-your-throat offensive philosophy and his smash-you-in-the-mouth defensive philosophy, totalled 304 yards rushing. They held the Trojans to just six total first downs. Ohio State outgained USC 360 to 206 yards in total offense with Howard "Hopalong" Cassady leading the way with 92 yards. Quarterback Dave Leggett, who was named the Outstanding Player of the Game, rushed for 67 yards and was 6-of-11 for 63 yards and a touchdown.

Hayes, meanwhile, didn't make many friends with Rose Bowl officials with his comments about the field conditions. The coach felt the field should have been covered before the game. He also wasn't happy with the fact that the bands were allowed to march on the field at halftime.

At any rate, the Buckeyes finished the season 10–0 for the first time in school history and captured its second national championship.

Another highlight of the '54 season came in October, when Ohio State dominated Wisconsin in a 31–14 win. The Badgers were ranked No. 2 at the time. Badgers running back Alan Ameche, who won the Heisman that season, was held to just 42 yards. Cassady returned an interception 88 yards for a touchdown in that game. In the following season, Cassady earned the highest collegiate honor as he won the Heisman Trophy.

Cassady culminated his career at Ohio State by winning the Heisman Trophy in 1954. *Photo courtesy of AP Images*

it 88 yards for a touchdown, giving the Buckeyes a 10–7 lead.

"I remember one game that year when Wisconsin came in as No. 1," said former Ohio State sports information director Marv Homan. "Ohio State was down early in the game, but they were hanging on. The Wisconsin passer threw a bomb and Cassady took it back for an [80-yard] interception return. That's the type of thing he did so often."

Former Ohio State radio announcer Burt Charles said about Cassady's game-changing plays, "He was a big-play player. When the marbles were up for grabs, he made the necessary plays."

With Ohio State clinging to a 10–7 lead heading into the fourth quarter, the Buckeyes put the game away for good with a 21-point fourth quarter barrage that knocked the Badgers out cold.

The scoring for Ohio State started with fullback Hubert Bobo going in for a four-yard touchdown early in the fourth quarter for a 17–7 Buckeyes lead. After Ohio State's defense stopped Wisconsin on the ensuing drive, the Buckeyes took over and quarterback Dave Leggett gave Ohio State a 24–7 lead midway through the quarter on a 27-yard touchdown run.

Wisconsin didn't help its cause on the kickoff as the Badgers fumbled and Ohio State recovered the ball at Wisconsin's 10 and on the very next play, Jerry Harkrader scored on a 10-yard touchdown run to give the Buckeyes a 31–7 lead. The Badgers finally scored a touchdown late in the fourth quarter to make the score

31–14. It was Wisconsin's first score since late in the second quarter when the Badgers led 7–3.

For the game, Wisconsin outgained Ohio State 357 total yards to 241 but the Buckeyes never gave up the big play and the defense, specifically Cassady, came up with big plays. And on offense, Cassady was effective running the ball. He led Ohio State in rushing with 59 yards on seven carries.

Ameche won the Heisman Trophy in 1954, but on this particular day, Ameche met his match in the Buckeyes. Ameche finished with just 42 yards rushing on 16 carries as Ohio State's defense came through, in front of 82,636 fans at Ohio Stadium.

> **H**e was a big-play player. When the marbles were up for grabs, he made the necessary plays.
> —BURT CHARLES

Game Details

Ohio State 31 • Wisconsin 14

Wisconsin	0	7	0	7	**14**
Ohio State	0	3	7	21	**31**

Date: October 23, 1954

Team Records: Ohio State 5–0, Wisconsin 4–1

Scoring Plays:

OSU—Weed 32-yard FG

UW—Levenhagen 18-yard pass from Miller (Wilson PAT)

OSU—Cassady 88-yard interception return (Weed PAT)

OSU—Bobo 4-yard run (Weed PAT)

OSU—Leggett 27-yard run (Watkins PAT)

OSU—Harkrader 10-yard run (Watkins PAT)

UW—Gingrass 1-yard run (Wilson PAT)

September 27, 1997

The Big Kat Finds His Prey

Young Linebacker Makes a Big Statement Against Missouri's Corby Jones

Andy "the Big Kat" Katzenmoyer came to Ohio State with a big physique and an even bigger reputation for being a brutal hitter as a high school linebacker. He had all the accolades that made him one of the top defensive recruits in the country his senior year of high school. And growing up in the heart of Buckeye Country, having attended Westerville South High School, just outside of Columbus, there was no doubt where Katzenmoyer would pledge his intent.

Ohio State fans soon saw that Katzenmoyer had the potential to be yet another in a long line of All-American Buckeye linebackers like Tom Cousineau, Chris Spielman, and A.J. Hawk. Early in Katzenmoyer's sophomore year, Ohio State faced Missouri in Columbia. The Buckeyes were ranked No. 7 in the country but Missouri featured the big-play ability of quarterback Corby Jones.

Katzenmoyer introduced himself to Jones midway through the second quarter with one of the greatest textbook hits in the history of college football. Missouri was leading 10–7, when ABC announcer Brent Musburger said, "We haven't heard much yet from young Katzenmoyer." It was as if Katzenmoyer's ears were burning, because on the very next play, Jones was rolling out looking to make something happen, as he had done for most of the game up to that point. Jones was scrambling to his left near the Missouri 25 when Katzenmoyer, coming at a full sprint, pasted his helmet right in the chest of Jones, lifted the talented quarterback off his feet, and drove him hard to the turf, flat on his back.

"There he is," Musburger said. "The Big Kat delivers the blow." Then Musburger's partner replied, "Man, did you hear the air go out of this stadium when No. 45 plants his helmet right on the No. 7 of his black jersey? Man, that's why he's going to win the Butkus Award for the best linebacker in the country. Nobody in college football hits like that."

What was Katzenmoyer's response when asked about the devastating hit?

"I thought it was big," Katzenmoyer said after the game. "And then I saw him lying there with his chin strap around his nose. I never did that to anybody before."

Andy Katzenmoyer first made a name for himself in an early outing against Missouri.

And Ohio State coach John Cooper said he had never seen a hit like that either.

"He almost killed the guy," Cooper said. "They didn't call him the 'Big Kat' for nothing. He could really close in for a 240- to 245-pound linebacker. He could close on the football better than anybody. He got a bead on that quarterback and it was just a great form tackle in the open field.

"He made plenty of highlight plays, but that had to be one of the best," Cooper said. "You don't win the Butkus Award and become a first-team All-American your sophomore year unless you're pretty good. But if you had to take out one play from his career and say it was the best, that would be it."

> **N**obody in college football hits like that.
> —BRENT MUSBURGER

Game Details

Ohio State 31 • Missouri 10

Ohio State	7	7	14	3	**31**
Missouri	7	3	0	0	**10**

Date: September 27, 1997

Team Records: Ohio State 4–0, Missouri 2–2

Scoring Plays:

OSU—Pearson 3-yard run (Stultz PAT)

UM—Jones 8-yard run (Knickman PAT)

UM—Knickman 27-yard FG

OSU—Boston 5-yard pass from Germaine (Stultz PAT)

OSU—Boston 28-yard pass from Germaine (Stultz PAT)

OSU—Wiley 1-yard run (Stultz PAT)

OSU—Stultz 28-yard FG

"Big Kat" was among the most fearsome players in the Big Ten.

No. 45

Andy Katzenmoyer wore No. 45 for Ohio State—a number that is legendary in Buckeyes football history because it was also worn by running back Archie Griffin, the only two-time Heisman Trophy winner in college football history. Griffin's number had been retired, but Katzenmoyer wore that number in high school and wanted to continue wearing it at Ohio State. Griffin graciously gave Ohio State and Katzenmoyer his blessing, and the number was unretired.

Katzenmoyer enjoyed a stellar career at Ohio State. An All-American and the winner of the Butkus Award, which goes to the nation's best collegiate linebacker, he even went on to play a few years in the NFL before a neck injury forced him to retire. Despite a storied collegiate career, it is his hit on Missouri quarterback Corby Jones that is still one of the more memorable moments for Buckeyes fans.

Interestingly, Jones later told the *New York Times* that the hit wasn't as big as it was made out to be. "First of all, it was a good, clean hit," he said. "But I didn't see him coming and Katzenmoyer knows that. Second, it didn't change the game. Third, I've been hit harder."

In the same *New York Times* article, Jones' roommate and then–starting tailback, Devin West, said, " Everybody kept replaying that hit, but nobody showed the 15 times in that game that Andy Katzenmoyer tried to tackle Corby and got a handful of air."

That may have been the case, but Katzenmoyer's punishing tackle was considered the turning point in the game by many OSU fans and objective observers alike. Before Katzenmoyer's hit, Missouri was leading 10–7. After the hit, Ohio State ran away with it, scoring 24 unanswered points for the victory.

A crucial part of the Buckeyes defense, Katzenmoyer was also clutch in special teams situations.

October 19, 2002

Madman in Madison

Chris Gamble Plays an Exceptional Game—on Both Sides of the Ball—in Last-Minute Win Over Wisconsin

Ohio State two-way player Chris Gamble was such a talented individual that Coach Jim Tressel couldn't just let Gamble play on one side of the ball. The Florida native contributed as both a wide receiver and a cornerback. In fact, Gamble was a *three-way* player for the Buckeyes, also playing as a kick returner.

With all those opportunities to make an impact on the field, it's no surprise that Gamble made a key contribution in Ohio State's run for the national championship in 2002, a 19–14 win at Wisconsin that came down to the last minute.

Coming off a big 50–7 win against San Jose State in Columbus the prior week, the Buckeyes were 7–0 going into the game. Wisconsin started out the season 5–0 but had faltered in their last two games, entering the matchup 5–2.

Playing against the Badgers at Camp Randall Stadium, one of the toughest places to play in the Big Ten, the Buckeyes were in a battle. Aside from a 47-yard touchdown pass from Craig Krenzel to Michael Jenkins on Ohio State's first possession of the game, all the Buckeyes could

put together were a pair of Mike Nugent field goals. Still, Ohio State only trailed by one point at halftime, and the score remained 14–13 heading into the fourth quarter, as both defenses held their ground.

Ohio State took a 19–14 lead with 9:59 remaining when Krenzel hit tight end Ben Hartsock on a three-yard touchdown pass. The score was set up by a nice fake on a run play by Krenzel. The Buckeyes failed on the two-point conversion, but the momentum was OSU's, after the impressive nine-play, 88-yard drive.

The Ohio State defense held Wisconsin quarterback Jim Sorgi to just 7-of-15 passing for 137 yards and a crucial interception. Sorgi was pressed into action after starter Brooks Bollinger left the game in the first half after suffering a concussion.

In the final drive for Wisconsin, Sorgi moved the Badgers down the field and was looking to move himself into Badger hero status if he could put together a last-minute, game-winning drive that would snap Wisconsin's two-game losing streak and, at the same time, snap Ohio State's seven-game winning streak.

Simon Fraser and Chris Gamble celebrate during game action. *Photo courtesy of AP Images*

Ben Hartsock pulls in the game-winning touchdown reception against Wisconsin in Ohio State's 19–14 victory. *Photo courtesy of AP Images*

Michael Jenkins

Most Buckeyes fans look to Chris Gamble's interception as the crucial play in the 19–14 win against Wisconsin, but Gamble's counterpart and equally talented wide receiver, Michael Jenkins, had a hand in the win as well.

Jenkins, who caught five passes for 114 yards, including a 47-yard touchdown pass in the first quarter for a 7–0 Ohio state lead, made a spectacular 45-yard catch to set up the go-ahead score in the fourth quarter.

"We just felt like we had to strike with some big ones if we were going to have a chance to beat them," Ohio State coach Jim Tressel said after the game. "A year ago, if you remember, we had some guys open and we did not hit them. It was good to see Mike come up with a couple of big plays."

Former Wisconsin coach Barry Alvarez said, "I thought the key play of the game was third-and-7 in the fourth quarter. They really hadn't done much for a quarter and a half and the ball was up in the air. We had two guys in position, no one made a play on the ball and they made a big completion and were able to go down and score."

The game-winning score was a three-yard touchdown pass from Craig Krenzel to tight end Ben Hartsock with 9:59 left in the fourth quarter that eventually gave the Buckeyes a 19–14 win.

Freshman running back Maurice Clarett set a school freshman record with his sixth 100-yard game. Clarett had 133 yards on 30 carries.

Unfortunately for Sorgi—though happily for Buckeye Nation—Gamble became the hero instead. He intercepted Sorgi's pass in the end zone in the final seconds, and it preserved Ohio State's win.

"He catches things better than most people," Tressel said about Gamble, who also caught three passes for 65 yards. "It doesn't matter if it was intended for him or if he was covering the guy. He can go up and catch the football. That was a pretty big one. He is just outrunning athletes, and you wish you could play him all the time."

> It doesn't matter if it was intended for him or if he was covering the guy. He can go up and catch the football.
>
> —JIM TRESSEL

Game Details

Ohio State 19 • Wisconsin 14

Ohio State	10	3	0	6	**19**
Wisconsin	7	7	0	0	**14**

Date: October 19, 2002

Team Records: Ohio State 8–0, Wisconsin 5–3

Scoring Plays:

OSU—Jenkins 47-yard pass from Krenzel (Nugent PAT)

UW—Davis 41-yard run (Allen PAT)

OSU—Nugent 27-yard FG

OSU—Nugent 25-yard FG

UW—Orr 42-yard pass from Sorgi (Allen PAT)

OSU—Hartsock 3-yard pass from Krenzel (pass failed)

Clutch Kicks
and
Special Teams Plays

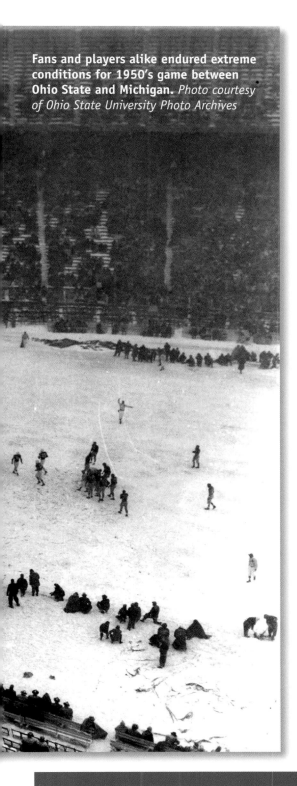

November 25, 1950

The "Snow Bowl"

Columbus Becomes the Frozen Tundra in Classic Matchup

Playing football in the snow is one of those winter pleasures—something kids, teenagers, and even adults like to do on occasion. But the 1950 "Snow Bowl" between Ohio State and Michigan wasn't one of those good times. The Buckeyes lost to the Wolverines 9–3 in a grueling battle. And it wasn't necessarily one play that decided the game; it was the conditions that decided the final outcome.

Players' toes and fingers were frozen, as was the playing field. So, too, were the 50,503 fans in attendance. As the Buckeyes' Vic Janowicz said after the game, presumably after his mouth had thawed enough for his words to melt out, "It was like a nightmare. My hands were numb. I had no feeling in them, and I don't know how I hung onto the ball. It was terrible. You knew what you wanted to do, but you couldn't do it."

Janowicz accounted for Ohio State's only points with a short field goal in the first half, which was set up after Bob Momsen recovered a blocked punt for the Buckeyes. The Wolverines scored on a safety after a blocked punt rolled out of the end zone for a safety then scored with less than a minute left in the first half when Tony Momsen, Bob Momsen's brother, blocked a punt then recovered it for a touchdown and the game-winning score.

Game Details

Michigan 9 • Ohio State 3

Michigan	2	7	0	0	**9**
Ohio State	3	0	0	0	**3**

Date: November 25, 1950

Team Records: Ohio State 6–3, Michigan 5–3–1

Scoring Plays:

OSU—Janowicz 22-yard FG

UM—Safety after blocked punt goes out of end zone

UM—T. Momsen fumble recovery in end zone after blocked punt
   (Allis PAT)

Neither team scored in the second half. Incidentally, the potential for a blocked punt was something that Ohio State coach Wesley E. Fesler and Michigan coach Bennie G. Oosterbaan were concerned about because of the horrible conditions. In fact, for most of the game, both teams kept the ball on the ground and punted on third down. The reasoning was simple: if there was a fumble by the punter because he couldn't catch the ball, he would still have fourth down to attempt another punt.

It was amazing that any points were scored at all when taken into account that 5 inches of snow fell before the game and the snow—as well as wind gusts of up to 30 miles per hour—continued throughout the game. Volunteers with brooms kept the sideline and yard lines visible as best as they could with their sweeping of the snow. It was reported that the storm was the worst blizzard to hit the city in 37 years. Ohio State athletic director

The weather conditions were so brutal that the teams were limited to just three scoring plays. *Photo courtesy of Ohio State University Photo Archives*

Dick Larkins didn't want to cancel the contest because trying to refund tickets to all of those in attendance would have been a colossal hassle. At the same time, cancelling the game—which was going to decide the Big Ten Conference and which team would play in the Rose Bowl—would have given the Buckeyes the conference title and Rose Bowl berth by default. Larkins, not wanting any of those aforementioned issues on his plate, was in agreement with Michigan and Big Ten officials in playing the game.

In the end, it all worked out in Michigan's favor as the Wolverines went on to defeat California 14–6 in the Rose Bowl.

> **It was like a nightmare.**
>
> —VIC JANOWICZ

Vic Janowicz

Six hundred eighty-five yards in one game. That's a feat that Ohio State tailback Vic Janowicz accomplished. But those weren't rushing yards, those were total *punting* yards. Janowicz punted 21 times in the "Snow Bowl" against Michigan.

Despite the fact that the Buckeyes hardly had an outstanding season in 1950—they finished the year with a 6–3 record—Janowicz won the Heisman Trophy by a landslide. His votes totaled 633 points; Kyle Rote of Southern Methodist was second in the balloting with 280 points and Red Bagnell of Penn was third with 231 points. At the time, Janowicz was only the third junior to win the award. During his Heisman season, Janowicz amassed 938 yards of total offense and scored 16 touchdowns.

Former Ohio State coach Woody Hayes, who coached Janowicz during his senior year, once said of Janowicz, "He was not only a great runner, but also passed, was a placekicker and punter, played safety on defense and was an outstanding blocker."

Janowicz's senior season in 1951 was Hayes' first year as head coach. Wesley E. Fesler coached the Buckeyes from 1947 to 1950 but resigned after the 1950 season because of the tension brought about by the tremendous desire to win football games.

Hayes welcomed the challenge—and the rest is history.

Vic Janowicz did it all in the Snow Bowl, including kicking for nearly 700 yards in the game. *Photo courtesy of AP Images*

November 20, 2004

Blown Away

Kick Returner Turns on Afterburners in
Staggering Touchdown Against Wolverines

"[Former Buckeyes coach Earle] Bruce tells us every year, if he wins the Ohio State–Michigan game, he can walk down the street in Columbus. If he loses, he better walk the back alleys. So it's an important game."

—**Jim Tressel, speaking to** *USA Today* **after Ohio State's 37–21 win at Ohio Stadium against rival Michigan**

With that said, Ohio State wide receiver and kick returner extraordinaire Ted Ginn Jr., should have marched a parade down High Street or Lane Avenue or Olentangy River Road—any street in close proximity to Ohio Stadium.

Having established himself as both one of the top football players in the country and one of the top sprinters in the country coming out of high school, Ginn Jr. used that exceptional speed to become one of the best collegiate kick returners in the country.

And on a breezy but mild November afternoon in front of 105,456 fans in the Horseshoe, Ginn Jr., a freshman, showcased his speed. Taking a punt at Ohio State's 18, he immediately eluded a tackler. Looking for an opening, bouncing and

Ted Ginn Jr. scorches
Michigan for six points.

The scene is set in the Horseshoe for another classic Ohio State–Michigan matchup.

dancing around waiting for a slight hole to burst through, he saw nothing in the middle of the field. Then Ginn Jr. bounced to the outside, turned on his afterburners, and sprinted down the left sideline, leaving every single player in the dust. Even on the Michigan sideline, all those players could do was watch.

Ginn Jr.'s return proved to be the game-winning touchdown as Ohio State took a 27–14 lead with 9:56 left in the third quarter. The Buckeyes eventually won 37–21.

"I had to try to make something real quick, and I was just trying to find a hole to get vertical, as my coach told me to," Ginn said after the game. "Once you see the touchdown, there's no point in making a move, you just use your speed and get to the end zone."

Michigan coach Lloyd Carr said, "Ginn's punt return was a major turning point in the game."

Game Details

Ohio State 37 • Michigan 21

Michigan	14	0	0	7	**21**
Ohio State	7	13	14	3	**37**

Date: November 20, 2004

Team Records: Michigan 9–2, Ohio State 7–4

Scoring Plays:

OSU—Gonzalez 68-yard pass from Smith (Nugent PAT)

UM—Avant 4-yard pass from Henne (Rivas PAT)

UM—Hart 1-yard run (Rivas PAT)

OSU—Smith 2-yard run (Nugent PAT)

OSU—Nugent 21-yard FG

OSU—Nugent 42-yard FG

OSU—Ginn Jr. 82-yard punt return (Nugent PAT)

OSU—Holmes 12-yard pass from Smith (Nugent PAT)

UM—Edwards 38-yard pass from Henne (Rivas PAT)

OSU—Nugent 48-yard FG

Ted Ginn Jr.

On January 8, 2007, Ohio State was set to play in the national championship game against the Florida Gators. The knock against the Buckeyes was that they didn't have the speed to compete against teams from the SEC.

That all changed in the first 16 seconds of the game. That is when a tall, lanky receiver named Ted Ginn Jr. blasted off like a rocket and went 93 yards with the opening kickoff to give OSU a 7–0 game-opening lead. During the end zone celebration, a teammate slid on Ginn's ankle, forcing him out of the game with a foot injury. The Buckeyes went on to lose the game.

When Coach Jim Tressel recruited Ginn Jr., Tressel knew he would be getting a gifted athlete. As a defensive back in high school, Ginn Jr. had won all the prestigious national awards—All-Ohio, *Parade* All-American, U.S. Army MVP of the Game—and was named the country's High School Defensive Player of the Year by *USA Today*.

During Ginn Jr.'s freshman year at Ohio State, the coaches decided to give him a shot on offense. His numbers weren't off the charts in his first year—25 catches for 359 yards and two touchdowns—but he was on his way.

"Here is a guy who came to us as a return specialist and defensive back and developed into a very good receiver," Tressel said of Ginn Jr. "He always had great hands and he became a very good route runner. With his speed, he was a threat to score anytime he touched the ball."

Ginn Jr. declared himself for the 2007 NFL Draft and was selected ninth overall by the Miami Dolphins. He wore No. 19 for the Dolphins in honor of his father, Ted Ginn Sr., who wore the same number in high school.

The touchdown was Ginn Jr.'s fourth punt return for a score, and the mark tied the NCAA record for touchdowns on punt returns in a season.

Meanwhile, Ohio State quarterback Troy Smith, who took over for Justin Zwick midway through the season, put together an impressive 10-play, 97-yard drive late in the third quarter that was capped by a 12-yard touchdown pass to Santonio Holmes. That score gave the Buckeyes a 34–14 lead. Smith also drove the offense 99 yards down the field for a touchdown earlier in the game.

"That is why I say you have to give Ohio State credit," Carr said. "The way we have always tried to play defense at Michigan is, if you have any kind of field position, the odds are you are going to stop them. We couldn't stop them. I think Ohio State played great [today]."

Michigan cornerback Marlin Jackson added, "Just like Troy, Ginn is an amazing athlete. He has everything a team could ever want in a player. He has the ability to make people miss like you saw, all year and today."

Smith was proud of the way Ginn Jr., his high school buddy and teammate, played against the Wolverines, but Smith said the win was important for the seniors.

"I'm pretty much at a loss of words right now because it's unbelievable," Smith said. "Coming off the field after the game, I almost got my neck [broken] by a lot of the fans. You know, this means a lot to everybody. Sending our seniors out was probably the most important thing that we wanted to do and we were able to do that."

> [Ginn] has everything a team could ever want in a player.
>
> —MARLIN JACKSON

Coach Woody Hayes gets his point across from the sidelines.

Skladany Scores

Beautiful Skies Help Hayes' Ace in the Hole Set Record

Tom Skladany is amazed that he still holds the record for the longest field goal kicked in Ohio State history: his unforgettable 59-yarder in a 40–3 win at Illinois. But the events that led up to Skladany's record-setting kick made his feat even more amazing.

"On Friday at practice, the day before the game, there was a 55-mph wind blowing through the stadium," Skladany remembers. "I was up all night with my roommate, Tom Klaban, who was also a kicker, worrying about kicking. He was up all night too." Skladany was worried because Coach Woody Hayes watched Skladany come up short on two extra-point attempts during practice because of that wind.

"I was kicking into 55- and 60-mph winds, and Woody couldn't understand that," Skladany said. "The wind just held the ball up like a wall. That's why [Klaban] and I were up all night worrying, because we didn't know what was going to happen the next day. I don't care who you are, you can't kick in 60-mph wind."

Skladany not being able to make his extra points didn't sit well with Hayes, but Hayes had to move practice along. So Skladany and Klaban were dispatched to the other end of the field while Hayes had the defense work on goal-line drills.

With Hayes' back to his kickers while he monitored the defensive drills, Skladany and Klaban were drilling 65- and 70-yard field goals with the wind—and making them look like chip shots. At one point, Hayes turned around and saw what was going on.

Was he impressed?

"Impressed," Skladany chuckled. "He yelled at us and kicked us off the field. That's how impressed he was."

On game day, Skladany was walking down a hallway near the locker room. There was a chalkboard installed at the end of the hallway so that players could see what the game-time conditions would be right before players went out onto the field. Skladany and the rest of the team had arrived several hours early, so they really didn't know what to expect at game time.

"When I saw the chalkboard, it read, 'Temperature 80, Wind 100 mph.' I thought, *That doesn't make any sense*," Skladany said. "So when I got down to the bottom of the steps, just before I went out onto the field, a guy comes

Game Details

Ohio State 40 • Illinois 3

Ohio State	0	10	10	20	**40**
Illinois	3	0	0	0	**3**

Date: November 8, 1975

Team Records: Ohio State 9–0, Illinois 4–5

Scoring Plays:

UI—Beaver 36-yard FG

OSU—Griffin 30-yard run (Klaban PAT)

OSU—Skladany 59-yard FG

OSU—Skladany 40-yard FG

OSU—Fox 20-yard interception return (Klaban PAT)

OSU—Johnson 4-yard run (Klaban PAT)

OSU—Johnson 1-yard run (kick PAT)

OSU—Logan 13-yard run (Klaban PAT)

over and erases the 1 and one of the zeroes. He said he was just messing with me."

Skladany breathed a sigh of relief, and once he walked onto the field, it was a beautiful sight. "The flag was draped straight down," he said. "It was 78 degrees in November, sunny skies, zero wind. The most perfect kicking conditions you could ask for."

Then came Skladany's moment.

There were two seconds left before halftime and Ohio State had the ball. Quarterback Cornelius Greene was sacked and the Buckeyes were holding a slim 7–3 lead. Assistant coach Ralph Staub said to Hayes, "Let's try to kick it."

Hayes replied, "That's too far."

Staub said, "It doesn't matter, there's only two seconds left and Skladany can do it."

Then Staub yelled, "Skladany!"

"It all happened so quick," Skladany said. "I wasn't even thinking about the distance, even though I knew it was a long kick."

Klaban had no doubt that Skladany could make it.

"In practice, we would screw around and kick 60- and 65- yard field goals all the time, so I knew that Tom could make that kick," Klaban said. "He was a straight-on toe kicker and I was a soccer-style kicker. Tom kicked with a low trajectory, so as long as it didn't get blocked, he could kick long field goals."

Skladany's kick wasn't pretty, but it was good. "I didn't really hit it good enough but it knuckle-balled over the crossbar. I didn't care, though, because it was good. It was just a perfect day to be a kicker," he said.

Klaban and Skladany were quite the platoon. One year before, Klaban had notched another school record for kickers, sending four field goals through the uprights against Michigan.

Tom Skladany

Tom Skladany was a three-time All-American from 1974 to 1976 and played in the NFL for six years, from 1978 to 1983. He was selected to the Pro Bowl after the 1981 season.

As much of a hero for his kicking prowess as Skladany was during his tenure at Ohio State, he also was humble. He said that with all the great kickers who have played for Ohio State, he feels blessed that his name is still in the record books.

"The funny part about it is, I should not have that record," Skladany said. "That record should have been broken two or three times since then, but no kicker after me has tried one that long. Think about it. Guys like Mike Nugent and others who kicked at Ohio State are the strongest kickers in the world. But because the situation never allowed itself, they never got a chance. And that's why I still have the record."

Skladany was known to have a wild and playful side. He said he got a kick out of riling up Woody Hayes at times. Skladany remembered this exchange after he was feeling good and having a great day kicking and punting at practice.

"Hey, Coach, you better call Columbus Metro Airport and have them reroute those planes," Skladany said.

"What are you talking about, Tom?" Hayes replied.

"I don't want to hit any of those planes,"Skladany said with a straight face.

Hayes just scratched his head and said, "Stay away from me."

Skladany went on to be a Pro Bowl kicker in the NFL. *Photo courtesy of AP Images*

October 25, 1919

"The House That Harley Built"

Versatile Ohio State Player Chic Harley Is the "Heart of It All" (Note: It's Ohio's Slogan) Against Michigan

Contemporary Ohio State football fans know all about the massive wave of scarlet and gray that flood the streets just outside of the legendary Horseshoe every Saturday during a Buckeyes home game. Fans gather in their Buckeye garb and travel from all over Ohio, and beyond, to make that pilgrimage near the Olentangy River.

The entire Ohio State football experience—from the "Skull Session" to "Script Ohio"—to the collective chant by fans that start from one side of the stadium—"O-H…"—then is answered by fans on the other side of the stadium—"I-O…—is almost a spiritual experience.

And one person, former Ohio State great Charles "Chic" Harley, laid the groundwork that helped turn Ohio State football into what is the "Buckeye Nation." Some say it started during the 1916 season, with Ohio State's 23–3 home win against Northwestern, as the victory gave the Buckeyes, who finished the season 7–0, their first-ever Big Ten championship, and Harley, a sophomore at the time, was the main reason.

Then, in November of 1919, Harley, Ohio State's first three-time All-American who played halfback, quarterback, end, kicker, safety, and punter throughout his career, set a school record that has yet to be tied or broken.

Chic Harley (shown here with the football) was *the* name in OSU football. *Photo courtesy of Ohio State University Photo Archives*

He registered four interceptions in that game as the Buckeyes defeated the Wolverines 13–3 for the first time in school history.

Harley wrote in the *Ohio State University Monthly*: "On October 25 was accomplished that which made the heart of every alumnus joyous- the defeat of Michigan at football."

And it was Harley's legendary athletic career at Ohio State, and his support of a $1.3-million stadium project, that led to the eventual construction of what has become Ohio Stadium, affectionately known as the Horseshoe.

In February of 1920, Harley wrote these words for the *Ohio State University Monthly* and they spoke to what Buckeye fans would say makes the Ohio State football experience arguably the most unique experience in all of college football:

"Maybe it's unconsciously, but somehow we go in there playing harder to win the bigger the crowd that backs us. There is inspiration, the finest kind, in the thousands and thousands of backers that a stadium like this one we're trying for gives room to seat…It's pretty hard to say in words what college spirit is but the team on the field and the crowd in the bleachers know mighty well what it

Game Details

Ohio State 13 • Michigan 3

Ohio State	7	0	0	6	**13**
Michigan	0	3	0	0	**3**

Date: October 25, 1919

Team Records: Ohio State 4–0, Michigan 2–1

Scoring Plays:

OSU—Flowers blocked punt recovery in end zone (Harley PAT)

UM—Sparks 45-yard FG

OSU—Harley 40-yard run (PAT failed)

is when the cheers are cut loose. I want to be there when our team trots out for that first game in the stadium—as an alumnus then, of course. I want to hear those 50,000 rooters roar at the kickoff. We're heart and soul for this stadium, the fellows who know what it is to go in there and fight with all that's in us for Ohio State and her glory."

Chic Harley is memorialized in a mural on Ohio State's campus.

The Buckeyes' First Superstar

Chic Harley *was* Columbus, even though he was born in Chicago. His family moved to Columbus when Harley was 12 but just before his senior year in high school, his family moved back to Chicago, but Harley, who got the nickname "Chic" because he was from *Chic*ago, stayed in Columbus for his senior year in high school.

He then remained in Columbus as an Ohio State Buckeye and he helped change the football program forever.

> **W**e're heart and soul for this stadium.
>
> —CHIC HARLEY

On April 21, 1974, Harley died of bronchial pneumonia at Veteran's Administration Hospital in Danville, Illinois, at the age of 78. Fittingly, Harley was buried at a cemetery just a few minutes from Ohio Stadium, on Olentangy River Road, and the pallbearers were Archie Griffin, Pete Cusick, Neal Colzie, Steve Myers, and Kurt Schumacher, all captains of the 1974 team.

"It was really an honor to be a pallbearer for the greatest player in Ohio State history," Griffin said at the time, with respect and humility. Griffin was college football's only two-time Heisman Trophy winner. "Chic put Ohio State football on the map."

During his career, Harley scored 23 touchdowns in 24 games, converted on 35 point-after attempts, and eight field goals, and finished with 198 career points. He played from 1916 to 1917 and 1919. He missed the 1918 season to become a pilot in the United States Army Air Service during World War I, but returned to play during the 1919 season. The Buckeyes compiled a 21–1–1 during Harley's career at Ohio State.

Harley's No. 47 was retired in 2004.

Harley was the unrivaled superstar on a dominant Buckeyes squad.
Photo courtesy of Ohio State University Photo Archives

September 28, 1996

Ready or Not, Notre Dame, Here We Come

Buckeyes Special Teams Make It a Special Win Against Irish

Dimitrious Stanley got the call—and came up huge—on a kickoff return against Notre Dame in 1996. He got the nod again the following week against Penn State (shown here).

"Lou Holtz [said] yesterday he's tired of answering questions about Ohio State... Did they invent football? Is this a coronation? Why doesn't someone ask me about my team? He said, 'I'll tell you one thing, the Buckeyes better be ready to play today.'"

—**National television announcer commenting on remarks made just before the start of the Ohio State game at Notre Dame**

And so that was the atmosphere surrounding the highly anticipated matchup between two of the most storied programs in college football history, the Ohio State Buckeyes, ranked fourth in the country playing at Notre Dame Stadium against the fifth-ranked Irish, Touchdown Jesus in the backdrop.

The Buckeyes were ready.

"To me, Notre Dame Stadium is just a stadium you go in to play," All-American offensive lineman and Heisman candidate Orlando Pace told the *New York Times*. "It's just an ordinary stadium. It's like

A Buckeyes player holds his helmet aloft in celebration of the win.

the Horseshoe. It's got 100 yards like any other stadium."

Both teams entered the early-season game undefeated. Another television announcer remarked, "It's a shame that these two teams don't meet on a regular basis." But to answer Lou Holtz's challenge, were the Buckeyes ready? It didn't take the packed crowd at Notre Dame Stadium long to find out.

Dimitrious Stanley and Shawn Springs were deep, ready to take the opening kickoff. It went to Stanley, who caught the kick at the 2-yard line. What transpired in the next several seconds was sheer delight for the Ohio State side and shock on the Notre Dame side.

Stanley started running right and it became a thing of beauty. If a special teams coach ever wanted to show his unit the most perfect example of how to set up a kick return the right way, this was it. Once Stanley got to the 15-yard line, the Buckeyes set up a wall of six blockers, including Springs, that completely neutralized and held up Notre Dame's five defenders on the right side. The blocks were sustained so perfectly that they allowed Stanley to hit a seam down the right sideline.

Then, at about Notre Dame's 45, Stanley cut back across the field and the footrace was on. Stanley was finally brought down by Irish speedster Allen Rossum, who was a three-year starter for Notre Dame and was a two-time All-American in the 55-meter dash.

A few plays later, running back Pepe Pearson went in from three yards to give the Buckeyes an early 6–0 lead, after an unsuccessful extra point attempt.

Was Ohio State ready to play? The Buckeyes put together 283 yards of offense in the first half compared to just 93 for Notre Dame. And Ohio State led 22–7 at half-time in a game totally dominated by the Buckeyes.

The win for Ohio State was a milestone in coach John Cooper's career.

"It doesn't get any better than this," Cooper told reporters after the game, and after he received the game ball from his players. "This ball was given to me by our football team for my 150th win. Obviously, that ball belongs to our football team and not John Cooper. But I am a happy man here today. I told our squad that this is a great victory for Ohio

> **I**t doesn't get any better than this.
>
> **—JOHN COOPER**

Game Details

Ohio State 29 • Notre Dame 16

Ohio State	12	10	7	0	**29**
Notre Dame	7	0	3	6	**16**

Date: September 28, 1996

Team Records: Ohio State 3–0, Notre Dame 3–1

Scoring Plays:

OSU—Pearson 3-yard run (run failed)

ND—Edwards 2-yard pass from Powlus (Sanson PAT)

OSU—Calhoun 3-yard pass from S. Jackson (run failed)

OSU—J. Jackson 24-yard FG

OSU—Pearson 1-yard run (J. Jackson PAT)

ND—Sanson 26-yard FG

OSU—Jones 13-yard pass from S. Jackson (J. Jackson PAT)

ND—Edwards 9-yard run (PAT failed)

OSU Defense Makes Statement of Its Own

As much as Dimitrious Stanley's 85-yard opening kickoff return was a statement for Ohio State, the Buckeyes' defense made a statement of its own against the Irish. Notre Dame quarterback Ron Powlus struggled the entire afternoon. He was sacked four times, threw two interceptions, and was just 13-of-30 for 154 yards.

"He was definitely distraught, really frustrated," Ohio State safety Damon Moore said. "We knew we had more speed on defense than they have on offense."

Ohio State entered the game ranked fourth in the country after trouncing Rice 70–7 and Pittsburgh 72–0. It was expected that Notre Dame would give Ohio State all it could handle. That prognostication never materialized.

"Their defense wasn't confusing," Powlus said. "They just beat us up….They were blitzing and weren't disguising it."

Notre Dame fullback Marc Edwards was just as straightforward as Powlus. "We embarrassed ourselves out there today in the first half," Edwards said. "The offense couldn't move the ball and we left the defense in some bad situations."

That loss against Ohio State wasn't the only bombshell for Notre Dame. Holtz resigned at the end of the season. He was replaced by defensive coordinator Bob Davie. The Irish finished the season with an 8–3 record and declined to accept a bowl bid.

But the reality is that Stanley's kickoff return was the spark that ignited the Buckeyes' fire. Stanley didn't score on the 85-yard return, but it was still one of the biggest kickoff returns in Ohio State history.

State, the players, and the fans. Not many teams can come in here and win against this great Notre Dame football team."

Stanley's kickoff was a statement made by the Buckeyes. It set the tone not only for the offense but for the defense as well, led by Andy Katzenmoyer and Mike Vrabel. The Buckeyes were in control of the game from start to finish.

"We come out and take the kickoff almost back for a touchdown, and that just set the tempo for the entire game," Buckeyes sophomore tight end John Lumpkin told reporters after the game.

Running back Pepe Pearson, who rushed for a game-high 173 yards with two touchdowns, said, "It felt great. We came in here and got the job done. You come in here to South Bend and beat Notre Dame, that's a great victory for us."

And there wasn't much that Holtz could say after the game.

"Ohio State is an outstanding team and played outstanding today," Holtz told reporters. "They are very strong up front. We didn't tackle great and they made some great catches and great plays. They have a nice offense and made the big plays."

To me, Notre Dame Stadium is just a stadium you go in to play.... It's got 100 yards like any other stadium.

—ORLANDO PACE

Wide receiver Malcolm Johnson hangs his head in dejection after the Buckeyes' defeat of Notre Dame.

Keith Byars simply dominated when he had the football. *Photo courtesy of AP Images*

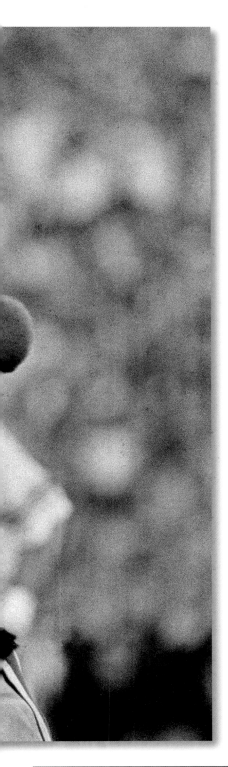

January 2, 1984

Going All The Way

Keith Byars Returns Kickoff 99 Yards to Help Buckeyes Defeat Pitt

There was something about the way Ohio State running back Keith Byars ran that looked funny. And the longer distance he ran, the more apparent his peculiar style of running became.

Byars was a strong, powerful, and physical back who could run you over or leave you in the dust. And in the open field, at full speed, Byars' feet looked like they never touched the ground. He used short, quick steps to accelerate.

Early in the 1984 Fiesta Bowl Game against Pitt, Byars scored on an 11-yard touchdown just before halftime to give Ohio State a 14–7 lead. It was unseasonably cold in Tempe, Arizona, that day, and the game lurched along slowly in the first half.

Pitt scored on a long drive in the fourth quarter that was capped off when running back Joe McCall took the ball near the goal line, then fumbled into the end zone where the ball was recovered by wide receiver Clint Wilson for a touchdown. That score helped the Panthers tie the score at 14–14.

That's when Byars stepped up and showed his impressive open-field speed. He took the kickoff at the 1-yard line, looked for a hole up the middle of the field, then turned it on. He came up with a spectacular 99-yard kickoff return for a touchdown. "They were kicking off, and I was like, *I hope they kick it to me, so I can make something big happen*," Byars said. "You don't forget things like that run. I'll be telling my grandkids about that play 40 years from now. You live for those kinds of moments."

Byars said people always discounted his speed because of his style of running. "I've always had speed, it was just deceptive," Byars said. "Guys didn't realize it until they started chasing me. Pittsburgh found out the hard way."

Although Byars' touchdown run was spectacular, the well-respected Ohio State leader said quarterback Mike Tomczak was to be commended for his play in the game, especially his play during the Buckeyes' game-winning drive with less than a minute remaining.

The game was fast and furious in the fourth quarter with the lead changing hands three times and both teams combining to score 30 points in the final period. Ohio State trailed 23–21 after a 37-yard field goal by Snuffy Everett with 2:39 left. Tomczak marched the Buckeyes down the field on an 89-yard scoring drive that ended when he hit Thad Jemison on a 39-yard touchdown pass with 39 seconds left to give the Buckeyes a thrilling 28–23 win.

"Mike Tomczak really stepped up for us," said Byars. "The media had portrayed us as a predominantly running team, but to see us pass the ball downfield like that with efficiency was really satisfying.

"The way we came back at the end of the game with the last-second touchdown pass was amazing," Byars added. "We just all banded together and it was definitely an Ohio State day."

Game Details

Ohio State 28 • Pittsburgh 23

Ohio State	7	7	0	14	**28**
Pittsburgh	0	7	0	16	**23**

Date: January 2, 1984

Team Records: Ohio State 8-3, Pittsburgh 8-2-1

Scoring Plays:

OSU—Tomczak 3-yard run (Spangler PAT)

UP—Wilson 6-yard pass from Congemi (Everett PAT)

OSU—Byars 11-yard run (Spangler PAT)

UP—Wilson fumble recovery in end zone (Everett PAT)

OSU—Byars 99-yard kickoff return (Spangler PAT)

UP—Collins 11-yard pass from Congemi (pass failed)

OSU—Jemison 39-yard pass from Tomczak (Spangler PAT)

Mike Tomczak had a lengthy career in the professional ranks, and even "shuffled" to a Super Bowl win with the 1985 Chicago Bears. He is shown here (left) with teammate Reggie Phillips.

The Running Man

Watching running back Keith Byars' spectacular 99-yard kickoff return, specifically during the last 15 to 20 yards before he reached the end zone, it almost looked as if he was going to run out of bounds inside the 10. And it wasn't because Byars was being forced out of bounds or the fact that he was being chased down by a defender toward the end of his run. In fact, by the time Byars reached midfield and broke toward the right sideline, he was running all alone.

But that was just it. Because no one was near him, he started to turn around and look at the rest of the players, his teammates included, that he left in his wake. And near the goal line, he seemed to almost tiptoe his way down the sideline before entering the end zone.

In fact, one of the television announcers said, "From here on, it's a footrace. And now he's worried

They were kicking off, and I was like, *I hope they kick it to me, so I can make something big happen.*

—KEITH BYARS

about, *What am I going to do when I get in the end zone? Am I going to dance? Am I going to jump? Who am I going to high-five?* And he almost stepped out of bounds. Oh boy. The excitement of college football."

The one thing that was interesting was that the run was so big for the Buckeyes that it seemed like the entire bench was in the end zone piling on one another. Naturally, that was long before the "excessive celebration" penalty came into existence in college football.

Byars had plenty to celebrate as a runner in the NFL.

September 11, 2004

Kicker Comes Through in the Clutch

Mike Nugent Becomes a Hero on the Last Play of the Game Against Marshall

Ohio State entered the 2004 season coming off a successful 2003 campaign. The Buckeyes were 11–2 in '03, including a 35–28 win against Kansas State in the Fiesta Bowl. In the first game in '04, Ohio State handled Cincinnati 27–6 in Columbus. But the following week at home, the Buckeyes found themselves in a competitive battle with Marshall.

The Thundering Herd tied the score at 21–21 on a 23-yard touchdown pass from Stan Hill to Brad Bates with 8:40 left in the game. The score had been set up by an interception of Justin Zwick.

Still, the Buckeyes had a productive performance from Zwick. He was 18-of-30 for 324 yards and three passing touchdowns. Future Super Bowl MVP and Pittsburgh Steelers and New York Jets wide receiver Santonio Holmes caught 10 passes for 224 yards and two touchdowns for the Buckeyes, an 80-yard score and a 47-yard score.

But even with those fine performances by Zwick and Holmes, Ohio State still couldn't secure the win. Marshall was doing everything they could to escape Columbus with one of the biggest upsets in its history.

Zwick threw another interception on the first play after Marshall's kickoff following Bates' touchdown and the Thundering Herd smelled blood. They took the ball down to the Ohio State 21-yard line, where the drive stalled. Ian O'Conner missed a 35-yard field goal. It was the breathing room the Buckeyes needed. It also helped that O'Connor got off a poor punt that gave Ohio State the ball at its own 45.

The Buckeyes were moving the ball down the field, but time was running out. With two seconds left, Buckeyes kicker Mike Nugent, a senior captain, trotted onto the field. He had the chance to be the hero and preserve an undefeated season. The fate of the Buckeyes rested on his foot.

Nugent was lined closer to the left hash mark for the 55-yard field goal. The ball sailed between the uprights with plenty of distance, and Ohio State had the game at 24–21. It was a thrilling victory.

"That's a long kick," Marshall coach Bob Pruett told reporters after the game. "I guess that's the reason he's an All-American."

Nugent's last-second kick against Marshall capped an emotional win for Ohio State. *Photo courtesy of AP Images*

But Nugent wasn't so sure the kick was good. "Every time I hit a solid ball, it goes back and forth a little bit," he told the Associated Press. "It kind of scared me at first. It was going dead-center and then it started going back in. I was just telling it to go in and that last second, it made it by about 2 inches."

The win was yet another close call for the Buckeyes, who had made a reputation of winning close games over the past few years. They had won 13 of 14 games over the last two seasons by a touchdown or less. "These [close] games happen so often here, it seems," Ohio State linebacker A.J. Hawk said.

> **T**hat's a long kick. I guess that's the reason he's an All-American.
>
> —BOB PRUETT

Game Details

Ohio State 24 • Marshall 21

Marshall	7	7	0	7	**21**
Ohio State	14	7	0	3	**24**

Date: September 11, 2004

Team Records: Marshall 0–2, Ohio State 2–0

Scoring Plays:

OSU—Holmes 80-yard pass from Zwick (Nugent PAT)

MU—Charles 2-yard run (O'Connor PAT)

OSU—Holmes 47-yard pass from Zwick (Nugent PAT)

MU—Goddard 27-yard fumble recovery (O'Connor PAT)

OSU—Hall 20-yard pass from Zwick (Nugent PAT)

MU—Bates 23-yard pass from Hill (O'Connor PAT)

OSU—Nugent 55-yard FG

Kicker Mike Nugent (85) watches his kick sail through the uprights as teammates Kyle Turano and Simon Fraser celebrate. *Photo courtesy of AP Images*

"NUUUUUGE!"

Mike Nugent's accuracy and consistency made him one of the best kickers in the country throughout his collegiate career. During his tenure at Ohio State, Nugent made 72 of 88 field goals, an impressive 81.8 percent, and he set or tied 22 school records. In his senior year Nugent won the 2004 Lou Groza Award, given annually to the nation's top kicker. In 2002 he became the first Ohio State kicker to earn All-America first-team honors after scoring a school-record 120 points.

Nugent was selected by the Jets in the second round of the 2005 NFL draft, 47th overall, and established career highs during the 2007 season with 29 field goals on 36 attempts and 110 points. That same year, he was selected by his Jets teammates as special teams captain.

Nugent was a star in high school, where he played alongside future Ohio State teammates Nick Mangold—who would also be Nugent's teammate with the New York Jets—and linebacker A.J. Hawk, a first-round NFL pick of the Green Bay Packers.

At Centerville, during his senior year in 2000, Nugent aced a school-record 52-yard field goal and was 29-of-29 on point-after attempts. In his high school career, Nugent made 13-of-17 field goals, a school-record 165 point-after attempts, and scored 262 total points. He also showed his versatility by throwing three touchdowns and running for seven touchdowns as a quarterback.

Mike Nugent accepts the Lou Groza Collegiate Place-Kicker Award in 2004. *Photo courtesy of AP Images*

Acknowledgments

The first person I would like to thank is longtime Ohio State sports information director Steve Snapp, for allowing me to develop the wonderful project idea that he came up with. It was an absolute privilege to be asked to do this book, and I thank Steve from the bottom of my heart and I wish him well.

To Paul Keels, the legendary voice of Ohio State athletics, *period:* thanks for lending your *voice* with your words.

Also, many thanks to D.C. Koehl, Ohio State assistant sports information director, for all of your help and support. Your assistance was invaluable.

Thanks to my friend and mentor, Jim Tressel, for the years of guidance that you gave me at Youngstown State, even when you didn't know you gave it to me.

Thanks to Deb, for running the Woody Hayes Athletic Center and getting me whatever I needed. I know who's *really* in charge at 2491 Olentangy River Road.

To the Buckeye Nation: I'm one of you and this book is for us. Growing up in the '70s in Warren, Ohio, and being a graduate of Warren G. Harding High School, I couldn't help but be an Ohio State fan. My dad went to Warren G. Harding with Paul Warfield and they played several sports together in their days and our families knew each other, so following the Buckeyes and the Browns wasn't an option for me, it was part of the fabric of my life at a very early age because of my dad.

Having grown up as a "Buckeye Nut" in Warren, it's such an honor to know that so many Warrenites went on to play for Ohio State, starting with Paul Warfield, John and Ernie Epitropoulos, Kelton Dansler, Aaron Brown, Tim "Bear" Brown, Van DeCree, Tyrone Hicks, Greg Zackeroff, Korey Stringer, LeShaun Daniels, Maurice Clarett, Vaness Provitt, Dimitrios Makridis, Daniel "Boom" Herron, and I'm sure I'm missing a few, and I do apologize. Sure, we had some outstanding Warren players who were a little confused and went to that school up north (Mario Manningham, Prescott Burgess, Carl Diggs, Alfie Burch, Dave Arnold, Tim Davis, Nate Rodgers, and Glen Franklin, I'm talking to you). I guess they didn't know any better. (Just joking guys—lighten up.)

Thanks to every single person in this book who allowed me to interview them because it was apparent that every player or coach I interviewed enjoyed yet another moment in their lives that they had a chance to retell stories that are forever etched in their minds. Those great, vivid, wonderful, and life-changing winning memories are what make Ohio State football arguably the greatest experience in college football. To Youngstown State, *everything*! I love you and always will!

To everyone else who helped make this project possible, thank you. You know who you are!

And to each and every one of you Buckeye Nuts, this is all that needs to be said, *"O-H...!"*